"WHAT IT SAYS"

From the Preface of *A Course in Miracles*

A Commentary

KENNETH WAPNICK, Ph.D.

Foundation for A COURSE IN MIRACLES®

Foundation for A Course in Miracles®
41397 Buecking Drive
Temecula, CA 92590

Printed in the United States of America

Portions of *A Course in Miracles* copyright 1992
Psychotherapy: Purpose, Process and Practice copyright 1976, 1992
The Song of Prayer copyright 1976, 1992
by the *Foundation for A Course in Miracles*®

Library of Congress Cataloging-in-Publication Data

Wapnick, Kenneth, 1942-
   "What it says" : from the preface of A course in miracles : a commentary / Kenneth Wapnick.
      p. cm.
   Includes index.
   ISBN 13: 978-1-59142-208-2
   ISBN 10: 1-59142-208-6
   1. Course in miracles. 2. Spiritual life--New Age movement.
I. Wapnick, Kenneth, 1942- II. Title.
   BP605.C68W367 2005
   299'.93--dc22
                                          2005029218

"WHAT IT SAYS"

From the Preface of *A Course in Miracles*

A Commentary

CONTENTS

INTRODUCTION

One year after *A Course in Miracles* was published in 1976, in response to requests for an introduction that could be handed out to interested people as a way of presenting the Course and explaining its origin, its scribe Helen Schucman agreed to write one. I no longer recall the details, but I think it was Helen who conceived the idea of having it be in three parts: "How It Came," "What It Is," and "What It Says." Helen herself wrote the first two,* while the third was scribed— i.e., dictated to Helen by Jesus—as was *A Course in Miracles*.

"How It Came" gives a very brief account of how the Course came to be written: Helen's relationship with William Thetford, and the scribing. The name *Jesus*, incidentally, does not appear at all, reflecting Helen's ambivalence about him. "What It Is" describes the structure of the Course's curriculum: text, workbook for students, and manual for teachers. Though not part of the official "canon" of *A Course in Miracles*, "What It Says" nonetheless offers a helpful introduction to the Course itself, providing a succinct overview of its theory.

The Preface was originally put out as a small pamphlet, and later inserted at the beginning of the Course when the second edition was published in 1992. For ease of reference, I have numbered the paragraphs of "What It Says" since it is not part of the Course's numbering system. Readers may thus wish to number the thirteen paragraphs for themselves.

I have often compared "What It Says," which for ease of reference I will usually refer to as the Preface, to a musical overture or prelude to an opera, in that it introduces many of the most important themes that are to be found in *A Course in Miracles*. I use the same word *prelude* that Richard Wagner used for his more mature operas, which he called music dramas. These preludes, which are similar to overtures, not only are symphonic summaries of many of the themes of his works, but they also establish the mood for what followed. And that is what we find here. Not only does the Preface present the most important themes of the Course, but it elevates the reader to the same level of thought and experience found in *A Course in Miracles*.

---

* Reprinted in the Appendix.

"What It Says" begins with a discussion of what I sometimes refer to as Level One, or the metaphysical foundation of the Course. Thus it sets the tone not only for the Preface but for what will follow in *A Course in Miracles*. Level One contrasts truth and illusion, knowledge and perception, God and the ego. It is the level that forms the basis for the Course's teachings on the ego's thought system—which finds its acme in special relationships—and its undoing through forgiveness. The Holy Spirit's correction of the holy relationship is certainly not understandable without a grasp of the underlying metaphysical foundation, which is that only Heaven is true, God is real, and our single reality is Christ, God's one Son. All else is illusion, without exception. The first three paragraphs deal with this Level One formulation, after which the focus of the Preface shifts to the dream.

In essence, the dream that is our life can be looked at in two ways—the ego's and the Holy Spirit's—and their contrast constitutes Level Two. The ego's thought system focuses on special relationships, which rest on the belief in scarcity. While we often use the term *scarcity principle* to describe the foundation of the ego thought system, the term itself does not appear anywhere in *A Course in Miracles*—only here. The words and concepts of *scarcity* and *lack*, however, are found throughout the Course. When our special relationships are brought to the Holy Spirit, they are transformed and become holy.

Like a musical interlude, Jesus next turns to the contrast between mind and body, emphasizing that the body does absolutely nothing but carry out the mind's instructions. In that sense the body is neutral, depending on the purpose given it: the ego's—to see separation and attack it—or the Holy Spirit's—to see shared instead of separate interests. The Holy Spirit's perception is expressed by the vision of Christ, and the Course's goal is that we share His vision of seeing everyone as the same in *content*, within which no one is different. Forgiveness is the means of undoing the ego's belief in separate interests, and when its work is complete and our guilt over the separation undone, we are in the real or forgiven world. God then reaches down and lifts us back unto Himself. The journey ends and we are home, where God would have us be (T-31.VIII.12:8).

The three-page "What It Says" thus offers us a summarizing integration of the Course's major themes and, line by line, we shall take the mini-journey through its beautifully written pages. I remember being with Helen when she took it down, and reading it hot off the "scribal press." I am not sure if I actually said to her, or simply had the thought, that she and Jesus had not lost their touch—this was a minor master-piece, expressing the same high level of form and content we find in the Course itself. I hope the reader will come away from this book with the same appreciation, if it is not already present. Let us now begin the prelude, as preparation for our greater journey through *A Course in Miracles.*

Chapter 1

LEVEL ONE: KNOWLEDGE AND PERCEPTION

The World of Knowledge

Paragraph 1

The section begins with a direct quote from the Introduction to *A Course in Miracles*:

> ***Nothing real can be threatened.***
> ***Nothing unreal exists.***
> ***Herein lies the peace of God.***

This is a Level One statement: Nothing real can be threatened since reality consists only of God and our true Self as Christ. In this context, I frequently quote from the text that "not one note in Heaven's song was missed" (T-26.V.5:4). In other words, nothing happened: God was not killed; His Son not crucified; Heaven not shattered. Nothing happened, because nothing real can be threatened. The corollary is that nothing unreal exists. Since *reality* is defined in *A Course in Miracles* as God, *unreality* is anything outside Him. This is a major theme in the Course, but not in the Preface, although it is expressed here. Heaven is a state of perfect Oneness, in which God's creation, His Son—His Effect, Christ—is at one with His Source. This means Creator and created, God and Son, Cause and Effect are not separate, for there is nothing to distinguish One from the Other. This means, too, that in Heaven you do not have terms like *Creator* and *created, God* and *Son,* or *Cause* and *Effect.* They imply duality, and there are not two beings in Heaven—only the One—and what seems outside perfect Oneness does not exist. We need always to keep in mind that this is a non-dualistic thought system that does not recognize as real what is apart from oneness. Consequently, anything of the physical universe—individual and differentiated—is outside the Mind of God and there-fore unreal. In understanding this, one learns the truth, for "herein lies the peace of God."

One cannot be at peace in this world if one believes there is a world. Our belief that a world exists manifests on a practical level in thinking the world has an impact on us. Thus, we would typically believe that our happiness depends on circumstances outside us: our feeling good about ourselves, or feeling loved and accepted depends on other people acting a certain way or treating us as our specialness demands. What the world calls peace generally means the quiet we sometimes feel when our needs have been met; or being peaceful at a given moment because we paid our debts, and so people are no longer angry with us—we completed our parts in the special relationship bargain. This is not to say the bargain will not be broken in the next moment or hour, or the next day, week, month, or year. This is inevitable in the ego thought system, at which point we have to make additional bargains. Thus there can be no peace as long as we feel the world has power to affect us.

Specifically, we experience the reflection of God's peace to the extent we are able to say that our happiness does not depend on anything external. The converse is also true. Our unhappiness, anxiety, depression, and guilt do not depend on anything external. Remember that in *A Course in Miracles* the body—ours or another's—is outside the mind. Therefore, if we feel ill, it is not because we have caught a disease. Both happiness and unhappiness, a sense of well being and discomfort, come from the mind, having nothing whatsoever to do with the world. Understanding this, and then beginning the process of accepting its truth, leads to the peace of God.

The reflection of these statements—*Nothing real can be threatened. Nothing unreal exists*—is recognizing that since nothing external has power over our peace, we are upset only because our minds made a decision to be upset. We simply used the world and body—specifically the bodies of others—not only as a means of justifying our dis-ease, but blaming someone else for it. This is part of the ego's plan to have us lose touch with the mind's power, which means our original decision for the ego remains intact. This mistake can be undone only when we recognize there is a mind that has the power to choose, and we have chosen wrongly but can now choose again. The world ensures this will never happen, because it says there is something outside, and peace is not achieved by choosing the teacher of peace—the Holy Spirit or Jesus —but by manipulating events, people, and circumstances.

This, then, is what we find in the Introduction to *A Course in Miracles*, and how Jesus begins this Preface, quoting verbatim from the Course itself. He continues:

This is how *A Course in Miracles* begins. It makes a fundamental distinction between the real and the unreal; between knowledge and perception.

This is a Level One statement that represents the all-or-nothing principle that underlies *A Course in Miracles*. It undoes the ego's basic premise, its first law of chaos: the separation is real and therefore there is a hierarchy of illusions (T-23.II.2). This "law" leads us to believe that some things in the world are valuable and others not; some objects, places, and people are holier than others. Obviously, the reverse holds as well. Certain objects, places, and people are less holy (or more sinful) than others. All this can be true only if the separation and the world of illusion—the perceptual world—are believed to be real. If, however, there is only the real and unreal, and the real is spirit, everything of form must be illusory. On this level, therefore, it does not matter what happens in the world. However, what does matter, as we will see, is how we *react* to what happens—which teacher we choose to be our guide in reacting to events and situations.

Knowledge is truth, under one law, the law of love or God.

If God is perfect Oneness, so is love, which is why love is impossible here. Yet, its reflection is possible, in the sense that we can love everyone in *content*—meaning we do not make significant distinctions among the different Sons of God. The world obviously makes such distinctions, as do our brains and eyes, but these are all based on form, having nothing to do with the underlying content. We are the same because we share the same delusional system that says we are here, as we also share the same need to escape from it, likened in *A Course in Miracles* to a dream. We are thus the same in sharing the one problem of believing in separation, and the need to undo it through forgiveness.

The vision of Christ, to be discussed presently, makes no distinctions among the seemingly different members of the Sonship. Once again, love, being oneness, does not exclude because it sees nothing other than itself. Even when people act in unloving ways—often hateful, cruel, and vicious—one can nonetheless see beyond the external sights of evil, and hear beyond the sounds of battle the call for love. Christ's vision, or the Holy Spirit's perception, recognizes that everyone in the world either expresses love or calls for it. In the end it makes no difference which it is, because our response would be the same—love. This is hinted at in these opening lines.

Truth is unalterable, eternal and unambiguous.

Truth is perfectly clear and unchangeable because it is one. The ego's fundamental premise is that the truth of God's Oneness has become dualistic—which means, of course, it cannot be the truth. In the ego's thought system, the Son is perceived to be in opposition to his Creator. The world emanates from this thought of opposition, which explains why everything in this world has opposites. Yet in reality, truth cannot be changed, cannot die, and is not complicated. What could be simpler than the statement: "We say 'God is,' and then we cease to speak" (W-pI.169.5:4)? "God is" is the simplest sentence possible, as English, with rare exception, does not permit one-word sentences. We, however, make truth complicated, as we see in almost all theologies. Indeed, some make this course complicated, yet it rests on a simple, unambiguous premise: truth is true, and everything else is illusory.

It can be unrecognized, but it cannot be changed.

Within the illusion—the dream of our delusional thought system—we can fail to recognize truth and love. However, that does not give us power to change it. To borrow from a statement in the text, free will does not mean we can establish our inheritance as Christ or change it; we are free only to refuse it (T-3.VI.10:2). This treasure is Who we are, although within the dream we are free to do whatever we wish with that Identity. We can thus choose to deny It—substituting the ego—but we cannot change the Fact of our Self.

These statements are not aimed at teaching about Heaven, which is meaningless and irrelevant to us who cannot understand it. However, what is meaningful and relevant are the practical implications of these abstract statements. On a personal level, we can learn to recognize how our relationships do not reflect these truths. Needless to say, relationships are complicated. Moreover, most do not last and all evolve and change. The changelessness of truth, however, is reflected in the love that is always present in relationships. This reflection is not eternal because it occurs in the context of one body relating to another, yet it reflects eternity because it does not change. One or both parties can choose not to recognize love's reflection, and may even try to attack it.

Yet, despite the ego's many attempts to express love—*special love*—we cannot change what it is.

Jesus asks us to see the unchangeable in the midst of the changing. This translates what would otherwise be statements having nothing to do with our experience into those that have everything to do with it. We understand the principle, and then reflect it here. Thus do these words come alive. Otherwise, we merely read them, regarding them as lovely thoughts, beautifully expressed, but they mean nothing because we will close the book and attack—physically, verbally, or in the mind. That could not happen if we took the principle with us and applied it.

We therefore set out to prove Heaven is a lie, and live its exact opposite: if Heaven is unchanging, we will demonstrate how changeable and fickle we are; how we love one day and hate the next; we like someone today and dislike him tomorrow. This has nothing to do with anything other than our whimsical responses to others. Yet we have already seen that the behavior of others is irrelevant, being of no real concern to us, just as our whims are of no real concern to us. Anything that changes is of the ego, and the only meaningful change here is the mind's change of teachers—from the ego's way of looking at the world and relationships to the Holy Spirit's. All other change is ultimately destructive because its purpose is to destroy love's unity. And so it is helpful when we read these statements about Heaven to see how our personal lives reflect that truth or its opposite.

It [truth] applies to everything that God created, and only what He created is real.

Remember, this Preface is like a prelude—not the full development of themes to follow in the Course, but a presentation of themes in part, to be heard later in their fullness. God can create only what is Himself: spirit, Love, Oneness. Anything that is not part of this Love and Oneness cannot be of Him, and therefore is not real. An important principle of *A Course in Miracles,* not mentioned here, is *ideas leave not their source.* Since God created us by extending His spirit as Christ—an Idea in the Mind of His Source—He has not left Him and thus remains part of Heaven's Oneness:

> ...nowhere does the Father end, the Son begin as something separate from Him (W-pI.132.12:4).

There is no demarcation point between God and His Son as there is in a dualistic system such as our world, where the function of bodies is to be separate from each other. Everything here is a projected thought or symbol, as are nocturnal dreams. Thus the body symbolizes the thought of separation, which says there is a beginning and an end of something that separates it from something else, which itself has a beginning and an end.

This process began when we believed we separated from God and took the tiny, mad idea seriously (T-27.VIII.6:2-3). Instead of there being the perfect Oneness of the Godhead—in which there is no differentiated God and Christ—the Son became a distinct entity in adverse relationship to his Creator and Source. Bodies are external expressions of that thought, for they have boundaries that keep them separate from other bodies and objects. In discussing the third obstacle to peace—the attraction of death—Jesus pointed out that death is a thought, having nothing to do with the body. He then issued this caution:

> ... neither sign nor symbol should be confused with source, for they must stand for something other than themselves. Their meaning cannot lie in them, but must be sought in what they represent (T-19.IV-C.11:2-3).

Similarly, we need to remember not to confuse the symbolic body with the thought of separation that gave rise to it. This thought is the source, which alone is the problem.

The message, once again, is to make these statements personally relevant by seeing how our lives reflect their truth. And when we see how we reflect the ego's truth of separation instead, to forgive ourselves. One reason we cherish judgment and find letting it go so difficult is that it is but another way of making the separation real. Judgment pushes others away, not necessarily physically, but in thoughts and words that give form to the decision to identify with the ego's thought system. Jesus does not ask us to love as God loves, but to reflect His Love through forgiveness. This undoes the separation that kept us from remembering It.

It [truth] is beyond learning because it is beyond time and process. It has no opposite; no beginning and no end. It merely is.

This is the essence of the statement I quoted above: "We say 'God is,' and then we cease to speak" (W-pI.169.5:4). Here Jesus adds the adverb—truth *merely* is; it is nothing else. It is beyond learning, which is why in the Course's Introduction, he says that

> the course does not aim at teaching the meaning of love, for that is beyond what can be taught (T-in.1:6; italics omitted).

And thus it is beyond what can be learned. It could just as easily have said it does not aim at teaching the meaning of truth. Yet *A Course in Miracles* does aim at removing the interferences to the awareness of love's or truth's presence (T-in.1:7). These consist of our special relationships, the various ways our lives manifest the ego thought system of separation. The Course's purpose is to undo them, and with these blocks gone, truth is merely left to be itself.

To repeat the point, the statements from the Preface are not intended to educate us about Heaven. They introduce us to abstract principles that become meaningful only when we apply them to our lives. Thus the text *and* workbook; the latter meant to be the mind-training aspect of the curriculum that asks us to apply the idea for the day—some aspect of the truth—very specifically. This is implied in the text and the manual as well, but the workbook, as part of its explicit methodology, asks us to use the lesson in our very real—for us—daily experiences. If I as a student do not do that, I am really saying I am not interested in achieving the state that is beyond learning. I am thus not interested in *the* truth, but only in *my* truth.

Truth is beyond time and process, which are not part of Level One wherein there are no steps, gradations, or hierarchies. On this metaphysical level, all time is illusory, as is space:

> For time and space are one illusion [separation], which takes different forms (T-26.VIII.1:3).

If there is no space, there are no bodies. Who, then, learns, undergoes a process, or holds Jesus' hand on the journey? Since none of this exists metaphysically, these statements about truth merely constitute the beginning of the Preface and only a small part of *A Course in Miracles*, the greater part of which, as here, deals with the illusion. On this level—Level Two—there is most definitely a process because we experience time and space, learning, and the need for a teacher. Yet in truth—Level One—there can be no teacher, because there is nothing to learn; in fact, there is no one to learn because no one exists outside the Mind of God.

A Course in Miracles is unique and impressive—not only as a spiritual path, but as a pedagogical instrument—because of Jesus' integration of Levels One and Two throughout, sometimes even in the same sentence. We are consistently taught that while this world is an illusion, we can yet live here according to Heaven's truths, which we reflect here. Thus we are not asked to deny our experiences, even though we are told they are unreal, without a hierarchy—no "good" or "bad"—for in the end, all experience is illusory. While that level of truth is not particularly helpful in our daily lives, it becomes essential when seen as a template in the mind we can reflect in our personal experience. If we follow that direction, we will not wind up denying our bodies as we journey home. Rather, we will deny the ego's interpretation of them. We will recognize this is not a journey to the cross— we are told in the text that "the journey to the cross should be the last useless journey" (T-4.in.3:1)—and so we will not deny our experience of process, only the ego's hurtful interpretation of it.

The World of Perception

Paragraph 2

The world of perception, on the other hand, is the world of time, of change, of beginnings and endings.

The world of perception, unlike Heaven, is the world of duality, which means time. We thus temporally experience a process with a beginning and an end. The word *process* clearly connotes change— you are not the same at the end of this process as you were at the beginning. The great process we all share is what we call life: we begin as a fetus, are born, go through various stages of development, and then die. This is the strange world of perception we think is real. Spiritual journeys, too, are part of the world of perception, and thus they, too, are journeys through illusion: "a journey without distance to a goal that has never changed" (T-8.VI.9:7). It is a process of simply opening one's eyes:

> The journey to God is merely the reawakening of the knowledge of where you are always, and what you are forever (T-8.VI.9:6).

Within the illusion of life's process, we speak of our spirituality as one of growth and change. It is not really like that, of course, but since we are not in touch with timeless reality, and are so identified with bodies and the thought system from which they arose, it is almost impossible to conceive of awakening as being anything but a process. Because our experience is spatial and temporal, the Course, in effect, joins us in those dimensions, and so Jesus speaks as if this process occurs over time—most notably where he describes the six stages of the development of trust, very much denoting a process that begins here and ends with the attainment of the real world (M-4.I-A).

In truth, again, process is an illusion. Yet since we see ourselves as children of the world of perception, Jesus teaches two ways of perceiving the illusion: the ego's wrong perception and the Holy Spirit's true perception, or vision—this constitutes Level Two, which we shall discuss presently. Both are illusory, being perceptual, but one deepens our involvement in the dream, while the other gently awakens us. Not only does the journey end when our eyes open, but we will not even remember there was a journey (see, for example, T-18.IX.14:1; T-19.IV-D.6:6). However, because we think of ourselves as bodies, the categories of perception will be meaningful to us—a journey of time and change, beginnings and endings.

It is based on interpretation, not on facts.

Early in the text, Jesus says that God is Fact (T-3.I.8:2). All other facts are illusory, including the fact of this course. Therefore, when we say the world of perception is interpretative, we mean we listen to one of two voices, what is subsumed under Level Two. Perception is interpretative because we interpret what we see through the eyes of the ego or Holy Spirit. The ego would have us see only expressions of separation, and so looking at the world and interpreting it—both the world at large and our personal world—reinforces the belief we are separate from God, and therefore from everyone else. Making the body real and acting on this belief makes separation real, too, since the body is nothing more than the projected thought of separation. Yet when we look with the Holy Spirit, we see what the body's eyes have seen, but understand that everyone is the same, despite the differences in form. We are not asked to give up our experiences or the categories in which we understand them—time, change, beginnings, endings—but simply to interpret them differently. By definition, there are no facts in an illusion, for if God's truth is the only Fact, all else is illusory. Again, there are no facts in the world, but there are two ways of interpreting the illusions we see: one breeds them; the other undoes them.

It is the world of birth and death, founded on the belief in scarcity, loss, separation and death.

Perception, in essence, is a synonym for *duality*—the physical world of birth and death. The body, therefore, is the great symbol of separation's inherent dualism. All bodily feelings and thoughts— positive or negative—along with decay, deterioration, and death, are ongoing problems for us all; not because of the body itself, but because of the ego's underlying thought of separation and change. It thus makes no sense to try to fix the body—not that you should hurt or neglect it—for to focus on the body is to focus on nothing. We rather want to use it as means to return to the part of the mind that chose the ego. In this sense the body can be helpful, for by demonstrating to us which teacher we chose, the body offers us an opportunity to change our wrong-minded decision.

The body's nature is to be in a perpetual state of scarcity or lack. There can be no disagreement on that, as we constantly need to fill our lungs with oxygen, our stomachs with food and water. The same is true psychologically—it seems we can never get enough love, attention, and devotion. Thus, both physically and psychologically, we seek to fill ourselves, which cannot happen without feeding off something else— an apt description of a more popular view of cannibalism. Remember, though, the body ultimately is nothing; and therefore it can be most effectively used as a way of recalling the thought that says we cannot exist unless we cannibalize, for the original thought that gave rise to our self was the cannibalizing of God. We fed off Him to take what we needed: life, love, and the ability to create. We took what we lacked, and the guilt that followed this horrific thought was truly horrendous. Since this is what the body represents, attempting to make it sacred or beautiful misses the point. The ego thought is hardly sacred or beautiful. As Jesus told Helen during the early weeks of the scribing: "The thing to do with a desert is to leave." In other words, do not try to improve the ego; simply leave its thought system behind.

The problem, therefore, is always in the mind, which chose to see itself as a murderer that destroyed Heaven so it could live. Consequently, the mind is where the problem's undoing must take place. Our sin is the origin of the body's perpetual state of scarcity and loss; the feeling that we will lose comes from our secret guilt that what we have, we stole, and therefore deserve to have stolen back. This also explains why we can never have enough love—no sooner do we have it than it seems to disappear. The ego tells us, however, that the love did not just disappear; it was taken. So we always have to get more, in what turns out to be a futile attempt to keep ourselves filled. That is guilt's role and, as we will see later, the role of the body's special relationships.

We all believe we will lose, because God had to lose at the beginning. Since the ego's reigning principle is *one or the other*, if God lost, we won. Yet, not for a moment do we think God is going to take this lying down. Even though we believe we destroyed Him, in our deluded thinking we also believe He will come after us to take back the life we stole from Him. This is why death is part of everything in the world, even inanimate objects; a rock, for example, may take millions of years to disintegrate, but remember that seventy or seventy million years are part of the same illusion. The body was made to die because the ego came from the death of God. Guilt says we stole and killed so we could live, and now God will do the same. This is the meaning of projection, and the body is the "living" testament to its efficacy. If we do not actively do something like breathe, eat, work so we can afford to eat, or shelter the body, we will die; and emotionally, if we do not get what we need from other bodies, we will "die" as well.

Even though the body represents the ego thought system of scarcity, loss, separation, and death, the body and the world in which it was born are not the problem. They are merely symbols of a thought in the mind. Again, *do not confuse symbol with source*. We want to undo the source, not the symbol. A symbol—to use Plato's concept—is the shadow, and a shadow is the absence of light, having no reality beyond its illusory self. If we do not like the shadowy effects of guilt, we need to change the source of our thinking. However, to manipulate or change the shadows, to fear or feel guilty about them, or attempt to breathe life into their nothingness is insane. The world is a shadow reality, as is a body, and our problem is only that we believe they are reality, not shadows.

To restate this idea, the world of perception is a world of lies. Perception tells us there is actually something we can perceive and know; something we can do and feel. However, careful examination reveals that the perceptual world is one of scarcity, loss, separation, and death. Thus it cannot be the world that God created. The world and body being unreal, therefore, means that our problems cannot be found there. Rather, the problem is that we *believe* there is a world and body. Beliefs are in the mind, the only place they can be undone. Again, Jesus asks us *not to confuse symbol and source*, which is the mind that has chosen to believe in illusion instead of truth.

A helpful line from the text states: "Nothing so blinding as perception of form" (T-22.III.6:7). One could just as easily say: "Nothing so deceiving (or false) as perception of form." Since everything here is perception of form, seeing you as a separate person attacking me is a lie, blinding me to what the problem really is: I believe the lie. Later in the Preface, Jesus quotes from the twice-stated line in the text: "projection makes perception" (T-13.V.3:5; T-21.in.1:1). The world we see outside is a projection of a decision we made in our minds. Therefore, if we do not like what we perceive, we need to change the decision. This means changing teachers from the ego to the Holy Spirit. We do not seek to change the external, because there is nothing there to change. Why bother to change a shadow, when all we need do is change the way we perceive it? Thus we read:

> Therefore, seek not to change the world, but choose to change your mind about the world. Perception is a result and not a cause (T-21.in.1:7-8).

To conclude the paragraph:

It [the world of perception] is learned rather than given, selective in its perceptual emphases...

Jesus says in the text: "You have but two emotions, and one you made and one was given you" (T-13.V.10:1). We could say one was *learned* and one was given us. God gave us love when He created us; our shabby substitute for Heaven's gift was special love—the one we made. We thus learned the ego's thought system that said fear is the reality and love is the lie.

Jesus' major focus in the early workbook lessons is to remind us not to be selective when we carry out his instructions. In Lesson 1, for example, he tells us not to exclude any object when we look around the room and say nothing here means anything. We are to be all-inclusive, but not in form, because we certainly cannot see everything. The point is that we not deliberately exclude something in our perceptual field. While Jesus refers to mundane things—wastepaper baskets, coat hangers, etc.—the training really has nothing to do with objects. We are being trained to be all-inclusive in *content*, even while we are being exclusive in *form*. This contrasts with the ego's world, which is "selective in its perceptual emphases," the meaning of the special relationship. We select those who serve our needs—either to cannibalize or to kill. In separating out who is helpful from who is not, it is not necessary to look at everyone. Thus we do not have to drink all the water in the universe, only what quenches our thirst. And so we need only be with those certain people who quench our thirst for specialness. However, by choosing them, we choose against those we do not want, thereby perceiving the Sonship as fragmented. Jesus thus teaches us not to exclude anyone from our love, for we would not want to exclude ourselves from his.

...unstable in its functioning, and inaccurate in its interpretations.

The world of perception is unstable. It is never sure, as are love and truth, but is always on guard because its life is built on the instability of attack and war—the killing of God and the resulting terror that He will kill in return. This battleground in the mind is first denied and then projected as the world. We thus end up in bodies, fearful and suspicious of all people, perceived as out to hurt, steal, or cannibalize. We suspect them because that is what *we* are doing, and since *projection makes perception*, we made them in our own image and likeness. Inevitably we look over our shoulders, keenly watchful of everyone and everything, never knowing from where the next attack will come because it is we who are always on the attack. Our lives are highly unstable, to say the very least.

Moreover, our interpretations of situations will be inaccurate for they are based on the ego. The essential point is that in the Course, *perception* means *interpretation*. It is not what our eyes see or ears hear, but how we interpret the data they bring back to us. *A Course in Miracles* helps us realize that the interpreter is not the brain but the mind, and the interpretations we make are those we want. The ego wants us to see separation, attack, and loss because that validates its thought system of separate interests, which gave rise to and sustains our existence. Again, nothing so blinding or deceitful as perception of form. On the other hand, the Holy Spirit's interpretation, to be discussed presently, is based on shared interests and common need, for He sees no meaningful differences among us.

The Two Thought Systems

This next paragraph remains on Level One, and contrasts the perceptual world of illusion with the truth of knowledge. Knowledge is not dualistic, in contrast to its popular usage, where there is a subject and an object: one who knows and what is known. When the Course talks about knowledge, however, it is almost exclusively used to denote Heaven—a non-dualistic presence of love—similar to the Gnostic understanding of truth (the Greek word *Gnosticism* has *knowledge* as its root).

Perception, in contrast, is dualistic: a perceiver and an object that is perceived, which includes our self-perceptions, for our bodies— physically and psychologically—are also objects of what we perceive and think about. Consider as well the biblical figure of God, Who exists in the ego's world as a perceiver, seeing His sinful children and acting in response to this perception. Even though the Course's language is borrowed from that tradition—the Creator is spoken of as a Person Who responds to the perceived separation by creating the Holy Spirit and the plan of Atonement, feels incomplete without His children, and weeps over their departure—the content is the opposite. The metaphoric language of *A Course in Miracles* is but a means to communicate in a context we can understand without fear. In reality, of course, God, Whose knowledge is perfect Oneness, does not know about the separation, let alone respond to it. If He did, He would exist in the dualistic world of perception, as insane as we.

Paragraph 3

From knowledge and perception respectively, two distinct thought systems arise which are opposite in every respect.

Jesus refers here to the thought systems of God and the ego: truth and illusion.

In the realm of knowledge no thoughts exist apart from God, because God and His Creation share one Will.

The key word in this sentence is *one*. No thoughts exist apart from God, and no Son exists apart from his Creator. This recalls to mind the line I quoted earlier: "...nowhere does the Father end, the Son begin as something separate from Him" (W-pI.132.12:4). This is the state of reality, the perfect Oneness that has no counterpart in the perceptual world. In the text, Jesus tells us that as long as we think we are separate, "the concept of a Oneness joined as One" is meaningless to us, yet it remains the truth (T-25.I.7:1). It is important at least to understand intellectually that this is the state of Heaven. Here, in the world of the split mind, we learn to reflect oneness by realizing we share one purpose and need; one thought system of insanity and one of sanity; one ego, one Holy Spirit, and one decision maker. In Heaven, we share one Will as Christ, and there is no distinctiveness within the Sonship.

Once again, though he couches his words in the dualistic terms of God and His Creation, Jesus makes it clear that reality is perfect Oneness—but another example of the linguistic compromises he must make. To speak to us of reality and oneness, he must speak within a dualistic framework. Thus he says in the clarification of terms that "this course remains within the ego framework, where it is needed" (C-in.3:1). The ego's framework is duality—words and concepts—even though Jesus tells us that salvation is the complete escape from concepts (T-31.V.14:3), "words are but symbols of symbols.... thus twice removed from reality" (M-21.1:9-10), and God does not understand words because they were meant to keep us separate (M-21.1:7). Therefore *A Course in Miracles* uses words and concepts, but for a different purpose.

Knowledge is now juxtaposed with perception:

The world of perception, however, is made by the belief in opposites and separate wills, in perpetual conflict with each other and with God.

Consider the ontological instant when we believed we were not only separate from God, but in opposition to Him with a will separate from His. In reality, this never happened, but the world rests on the belief it did. In that instant, the Son looked at himself in relation to his Creator and said, in effect: "I am not happy with the situation in which

I am second; I do not want to be subjugated to You." Separate wills inevitably lead to perception of opposing wills. Within the split mind, once we believe in separation we must believe there are differences, which are established and protected by attack. Thus has judgment replaced love as the truth.

Separation, differentiation, judgment, and attack are the same. If we have one, we have the others, which means from the moment we believe we are separate from God, we also believe we are in opposition to Him. We make differences real, judge them, and attack to protect what we now think we have. We believe that the separated self opposed to God is our own, and defend to the death its right to exist. We kill everyone and everything—if not physically, then certainly in our thoughts. We kill by using, seducing, manipulating, and cannibalizing, relating to people out of selfish rather than shared interests. We do not care about others, but only how they can meet our needs. Such actions began with the insane thought we believed was reality, in which we selfishly said to our Creator: "I do not care about You or Your perfect Oneness and Love. I care only about me." Our horrific guilt over that statement set into motion the ego's delusional system that culminated in the making of the world.

Yet if *ideas leave not their source,* the world has never left the mind's thought of separation. Everything here derives from the idea that we exist because we stole from God, and now have to protect ourselves so He does not return the compliment. Remember, however, that these concepts but symbolically express the Course's myth of the ego. This myth explains how each of us lives in the world—always on the defensive, doing anything necessary to protect what we have stolen. Consequently, we are angry and judgmental, yet often attempt to camouflage our judgments by acting otherwise. The fact remains we were conceived in hate—hating our Source because of what we believed He withheld from us: autonomy, independence, and freedom. When God did not grant us the separate self our specialness demanded, we made it ourselves. The body then came to embody—if not glorify—that hateful self, for it asserts our existence as separate entities. A wall surrounds this self—physically and emotionally—that says to the world, including God: "Thou shalt not enter here! But if you do, it will only be so I can cannibalize you, get what I want, and cast you out." We do the same thing to each other. Moreover, we know others do it back to us because we did it first, and they do not exist outside our deluded minds.

Everything here is predicated on the belief in separate wills, in perpetual conflict with each other because they are in conflict with God. We are also in perpetual conflict with the environment, for we cannot exist without having water, oxygen, and food. Nations are in conflict with each other as well, because no one nation has all the natural resources, food, and goods it needs. This gives rise to trade, which is almost never based on shared interests but on each nation getting as much as it can, while giving as little as possible in return. It must be so, because this is what we did with God, making a bargain with Him that if only He would spare us, we would recompense Him.

Once again, understanding this myth of our conflict with God helps us see what we manifest in our special relationships, to be discussed below. Moreover, recognizing their origin in the mind of God's Son—each of us being a fragment of the one Son and his two thought systems—allows us to see how we are all the same. In addition, if we understood that *ideas leave not their source*, and that the source is the insanity of the ego, we would have sympathy for everyone—being alike, we are all in the same miserable boat. This is clear, once again, when we see how in order to stay alive, we need to cannibalize oxygen, water, and food, to say nothing of psychologically cannibalizing love and approval. In sum, we come from the same source: in truth, God; in illusion, the ego.

What perception sees and hears appears to be real because it permits into awareness only what conforms to the wishes of the perceiver.

The word *body* has not yet appeared in the Preface, but there can be no perception without it. Perception appears real because we made the body with a sophisticated network of sensory apparatus that perceives data presumed to be external, brings those data to where the brain—also part of the body—interprets them and gives messages to us to act accordingly. We do not realize that all this activity is orchestrated by the mind, not the brain's complicated neurological and sensory system. The body functions solely for the purpose of proving the separation real—it sees, hears, tastes, feels, smells, and intuits things. Whether you are talking about the five senses or a sixth one, it remains all about separation by proving that the body and world are real.

We are not aware that perception reflects a secret wish. Not only is the world an outside picture of an inward condition (T-21.in.1:5), but

21

perception is an outside picture of the mind's wish to make the separation real, yet project all responsibility for it. In the perceptual world, bodies exist solely to prove we separated from God, differentiation is a fact, and judgment and attack are justified: look how we suffer at the hands of others.

Freud held that dreams are fulfillments of wishes, exactly what Jesus says here, although on a much larger scale. Everything is a wish fulfillment, not just our sleeping dreams. That unconscious wish is the wish to be separate, but not to be responsible for it. Thus I think: if my body is in pain, it is not due to my mind's decision, but because I was invaded by bacteria, ate spoiled food, did not get enough clean air to breathe, lacked love and attention, or my body obeyed the natural laws of aging. I therefore attribute pain to any or all of these types of causes, but not to a decision my mind made to be guilty:

> Of all the many causes you perceived as bringing pain and suffering
> to you, your guilt was not among them (T-27.VII.7:4).

Even further, we claim that physical life begins with a totally innocent and helpless fetus that continues as an infant, also innocent and helpless, at the mercy of forces beyond its control. What better way to fulfill the ego's secret wish, conforming to the perceiver's wishes? For the baby's life proclaims: "I exist, but it is not my doing. It was not my decision to be born, to be hungry, have diaper rash, or be rejected. I cannot take care of myself." This statement is clearly the ego's giveaway when we move beyond the symbol to the source; beyond the form to the content. Whether we are one-day old, or forty, fifty, or ninety years old, this does not change. We are all babies, possessing one all-consuming mouth that says: "Feed me; and if you do not, I will let you and the world know it."

Everyone understands this because we are of the same body, representing the ego's same secret wish. Such awareness helps pull together the seemingly disparate elements of our experience, because our lives follow the same wrong-minded path. All life here conforms to the secret wish, and fulfills it beautifully from the ego's point of view. Bodies cannot exist without something external to keep them going, which, again, exposes the ego's strategy. If this is a dream, why did we make a body that is not self-sufficient and needs things from the outside? The answer is simple: that is the thought's origin—I need God's Love and thus must feed off Him; I have to steal His power because I have nothing. Since mind and body are of one piece, the body is merely a shadow of the original thought: an illusory thought that led to an illusory world, yet never left its source.

Again, it is helpful to see how this secret wish—the separation is real, but I am not responsible for it—plays out in the specifics of our everyday lives, wherein everything is designed to prove that the way we feel is attributable to someone or something else. If we awaken in the morning and do not feel well, we have a host of causes to blame: we are ill or troubled; it was something we ate, a change in weather, a meeting we are dreading; or we had a bad dream—none of which has anything to do with the mind, except to be its effect. In other words, the ego enables us to conclude that the separation from God is made real by the laws of perception, but is not our doing.

This leads to a world of illusions, a world which needs constant defense precisely *because* it is not real.

This is a pertinent statement. Anger, hatred, or judgment on any part of the ego's continuum of specialness is defensiveness. When you experience God's Love, there is no need to defend anything because you know you are not separate from Him. When you feel Jesus' presence, the symbol of God's Love within the dream, you know you are not separate from him. This means there is no sin, guilt, fear of punishment, or projection, and therefore no need to be defensive.

We defend only illusions. When people say they want to protect their religious faith from the infidels—whether they mean the Bible or *A Course in Miracles*—you know they no longer speak from an experience of the Love of God, but from the love of their ego god, which definitely needs protection and defense. *A Course in Miracles* does not need people to stand up for it, nor to teach and proclaim its truth. You *are* the truth; therefore your very presence is the teacher. Whenever you seek to defend something—yourself from another, or an ideal you believe in, such as the Course—you are defending illusions. In the presence of truth and love, there is nothing to protect because nothing is endangered.

The ego thought system began with the lie that something terrible happened to God. Not only was one note missed in Heaven's song when the impossible happened, the whole symphony was destroyed—God was annihilated, His Son crucified, and the love of Heaven obliterated. At least that is what the ego told us. Something happened, which necessitated a reaction that cleverly gave rise to defenses. An important line in the text states: "Defenses *do* what they would defend" (T-17.IV.7:1). The purpose of a defense is to protect us from fear, which attests that something is going to be done to us because we did something first; i.e., we sinned. The overt purpose of a defense is to protect us, but all it does is confirm that something can hurt us because we hurt something else. Defenses, thus, reinforce the very thought of sin that is the cause of fear. They *do* what they defend; but all we ever defend is an illusion.

Again, truth needs no defense; neither does God, Jesus, or his course. *We* do not need a defense. That is the message of the wonderful lesson: "In my defenselessness my safety lies" (W-pI.153). If I am in a defensive posture—the ego's perpetual state—I reinforce the fact of my vulnerability. Therefore, how can I be safe? Perhaps I can protect myself from the enemy over here, but how about the one over there? Or the one tomorrow? If we do not undo guilt, we do not undo the source of fear. Guilt stems from the premise that something sinful occurred: God's Love was shattered, and we did it! All we need do to prove this is reality is to make separation real in some form—to see ourselves as separate from another. On the other hand, all we need do to correct this error is see our interests as the same as another's. Separation then disappears, which means there is no guilt, projection, or fear—consequently, there is no need for defenses. We can thus say that the dream's reflection of Heaven's innocence is defenselessness— the conviction there is nothing we have to do to protect ourselves or anyone else. Moreover, it is essential to remember that none of this pertains to form or behavior, only to content or thought.

This concludes our discussion of Level One. The remainder of the Preface is presented within the framework of Level Two.

Chapter 2

LEVEL TWO: THE WORLD OF PERCEPTION –
THE EGO AND THE HOLY SPIRIT

Level One, as we have seen, contrasts truth and illusion, knowledge and perception. Level Two deals only with illusion and perception—the dream. This level contrasts the ego's wrong-minded perception, separate interests, and the Holy Spirit's right-minded perception, shared interests. Both are illusory; but wrong-minded perceptions of guilt reinforce and lead to further illusions, while right-minded perceptions of forgiveness undo them. When forgiveness has undone guilt, both disappear, as do the ego and Holy Spirit. This is the state known as the real world, with which the Preface essentially ends.

Having made his point that understanding knowledge is beyond our capacity as separated minds, Jesus sets knowledge aside. While love and oneness will never be understood here, their reflections can be learned, practiced, and experienced through perceiving everyone with the same needs, problems, and goals. Thus do we escape from the ego's dream of separation and perception.

Escape from the Dream

Paragraph 4

When you have been caught in the world of perception you are caught in a dream.

One of the primary analogies Jesus uses to teach about the illusory world of perception is the dream. When he says we are "at home in God, dreaming of exile" (T-10.I.2:1), he could also have said we are awake in God, dreaming of exile. The dream is a helpful symbol because it is one with which everyone is familiar. Freud built psychoanalysis upon his understanding of dreams, and then generalized it. Jesus, in essence, does the same thing. As I mentioned earlier, he expands the concept of the sleeping dream to the world itself as a dream. We all more or less understand the nature of nocturnal dreams—how real they seem while we sleep, and how unreal they suddenly become when we awake. This can be extrapolated to all our experiences. While we are awake—or think we are—the world seems very real, and we think events actually happen. Yet that is hardly the case, for the world occurs only in the mind. Therefore, as we go through the day, experiencing the world as truly there, we need to remember the dream and how our sleeping dreams appear to be so real. This will help us not take our lives quite as seriously as before.

An intellectual understanding of the nature of dreaming is the first step in the process of integrating the principle experientially, and you will know you are advancing in that direction when you no longer give the world power over you. You certainly do not deny or dismiss what goes on, nor are you cavalier or insensitive about events. However, you would no longer see them as able to take away your peace, which is the meaning of seeing the world as an illusion. To restate the point, you do not deny there is a world, but you deny that the world is the cause of your dis-ease or lack of peace. It indeed has power over your body, which can be made to feel pain and even destroyed, yet the world has no effect on your mind. Its power rests only within the dream, and while your mind dreams of separation, the world can certainly make you anxious, angry, depressed, sick, or happy, but as your eyes open, the dream fades and you realize it had no true power at all. Faded, too, is the intensity behind solving an illusory problem that beforehand had been a major focus of your attention. This lack of need frees you to be more effective as you relate to the world, for with conflict gone, the tension that interferes with everyday functioning is gone as well.

We are therefore asked to begin the process of seeing that the world is powerless to take away our peace. No matter what is done around us, or to people we know and love, it can have no effect on us unless we give it that power. Recall the important line that speaks about the figures in the dream:

> Let them be as hateful and as vicious as they may, they could have no effect on you unless you failed to recognize it is your dream (T-27.VIII.10:6).

However merciless the world, it can affect us only if we forget it is a dream. When we remember, nothing here can change our inner peace. Thus people survive traumatic situations in the world—physically and psychologically—not through denial, but through recognizing: "This has nothing to do with me. It might have something to do with my body and the bodies of my loved ones; but it has nothing to do with my mind, which is who I am." Such recognition takes much work and practice, but as we do so, we at least know we are in the right classroom with the right teacher. Perhaps we are still in kindergarten, nursery, or even pre-nursery school; *but we are in school.* Our lives, therefore, have great meaning. We have the assurance that life is meaningful because we are truly learning. Having chosen the right teacher, who helps us use everything as his classroom, we learn that who we are is totally unaffected by what goes on around us, and that not one note in our song is missed by what the world does. Our song of forgiveness thus happily reflects Heaven's song of love.

You cannot escape without help...

To quote from the beginning of the text, the ego thought system is "fool-proof" (T-5.VI.10:6), which means that once we are in the ego system, there is no way out from within that system. The very skills, abilities, ingenuities, and strengths that have gotten us through difficult times in our lives—through school, relationships, and work experiences—prevent us from awakening from the dream. They have helped us survive *in* the dream, but not helped us awaken *from* it. If we therefore continue to rely on these strengths and abilities, we end up relying on ourselves. In short, we need help that comes from outside the ego.

...because everything your senses show merely witnesses to the reality of the dream.

It is not only what our senses show that is the problem, but what our brains do with what our senses show. We have all learned more or less how to survive and have our needs met. We receive data from the world, analyze them, and develop a plan of action. Some people seem better at this than others, but we all somehow manage. In the womb, we do nothing on our own, but at birth our bodies quickly learn to adapt to our strange and hostile environment. As we grow, we learn to breathe, eat, and take care of ourselves; how to deal with the world physically and psychologically. Indeed, it is vital that we learn, otherwise we will never emerge from childhood into adulthood.

All this is a necessary part of the classroom in which we eventually learn we do not have to rely on ourselves to awaken from the dream. We certainly have had to rely on ourselves to live here, but to awaken we need help from outside the system—outside the body and brain. Even though the ego thought system is fool-proof, it is not God-proof (T-5.VI.10:6). God, truth, reality, and love are outside the ego; yet the memory of God remains within the split mind as the Holy Spirit—the memory of the reality we believe we not only left, but destroyed, and which is now hell-bent on destroying us. Thus, we need the help, because everything our "senses show merely witnesses to the reality of the dream."

We can speak of Jesus as the light that shines in our minds from outside the dream, calling to us to leave it. We experience his love in the body, but only so it will lead us beyond it to the mind. Unfortunately, the world brought him into the body's dream, making him a part of it. However, as he told Helen: "I am not a dream that comes in mockery" (*The Gifts of God*, p. 121), meaning he is not part of the dream that mocks the creation of God. He thus invites us to take his thought that symbolizes reality, and follow it as it leads us out of the dream *to* reality.

God has provided the Answer, the only Way out, the true Helper.

Note the Course's dualistic language, which we now revisit. God has not literally provided the answer, for if He did, He would have recognized there was a problem. This would mean we have an even bigger problem, as God would be sharing our insanity in seeing what does not exist. That is why the biblical God is so erratic, having both good and bad days. His instability is inevitable because it comes from the ego's unstable thought. Thus has our Source been dragged into the dream as a perceptual God Who sees sin and judges it, and then develops an horrific plan that concludes with His giving Jesus to the world as a sacrifice. And so consider the biblical myth we all grew up with. It focuses on God's wrath, vengeance, and the last judgment, and Heaven will *not* help you if you are an Egyptian, a money changer in the temple, a scribe or Pharisee, a goat, or a thief on the wrong side of the cross. This God is unmistakably selective in His forgiveness, mercy, and love. Whether or not you formally believe in God, you do believe in a myth that says: I sinned, truth notices, and it responds in kind. This expresses the sinful condition we think we are in, which reflects the second and third laws of chaos: the Son tells the Father he has sinned, the Father believes him, and He practices atonement with vengeance (T-23.II.4-8).

Clearly, this is not the God of *A Course in Miracles*, Who transcends the dualistic world entirely. However, since the world's notion of God is essentially the biblical figure, Jesus uses the familiar language and speaks of the Creator as if He were a member of homo sapiens. In truth, of course, God is not a person, but we must think He is because we think we are:

> Can you who see yourself within a body know yourself as an idea? Everything you recognize you identify with externals, something outside itself. You cannot even think of God without a body, or in some form you think you recognize (T-18.VIII.1:5-7).

We should therefore not be confused by the Course's language, but should read it as we would an epic poem that contains a magnificent set of symbols. Again, we need be careful not to confuse symbol with source, words with reality. Symbols should be used as a way of helping us move beyond them, as we are instructed to do in "Beyond All Symbols" (T-27.III). *A Course in Miracles* is merely a set of symbols, used to meet us where we think we are in the dream, so we can awaken from it; but the symbols are not true in themselves.

I earlier referred to the passage that stated that "the concept of a Oneness joined as One" is one we can never understand (T-25.I.7:1). Jesus goes on to say that Oneness has to speak to us in the condition in which we think we exist:

> Yet must It use the language that this mind can understand, in the condition in which it thinks it is (T-25.I.7:4).

This condition is separation and duality, and so the oneness of Heaven's love speaks to us in symbols that reflect our dualistic condition. The Course's language, therefore, has a specific purpose, which is in harmony with the Holy Spirit's purpose. As we will see later, the Holy Spirit does not take away our special relationships, but transforms them. So, too, Jesus does not take away our dualistic language; he transforms it.

Jesus thus makes up a story using the same elements of the ego's myth: we sinned, God noticed, and He responded. However, this myth has a gentle meaning that is not frightening, for our loving brother Jesus is tucking us in bed, telling us a kindly fairy tale. It is the story the ego told us night after night—the same scenario and set of characters, but with a totally different content. God's answer is not Atonement with our sacrifice, for it does not reinforce guilt, or rest on the principle of *one or the other* where one has to suffer and die because of our sin. Jesus' fairy tale is therefore not meant to be literal truth, but a right-minded correction for the ego's wrong-minded story. *A Course in Miracles* teaches us that the ego speaks first, is wrong, and the Holy Spirit is the Answer (T-5.VI.3:5; 4:1-2). This course is thus the answer to the ego. Its tale of sin, guilt, fear, God's punitive wrath, and our suffering and death is corrected by our older brother, who lovingly leads us from the ego's nightmare world to our home.

It is the function of His Voice, His Holy Spirit, to mediate between the two worlds.

In truth, the Holy Spirit is a thought—a memory of God's Love and our Identity as Christ—which we took with us into the dream when we fell asleep. If we think of the Holy Spirit in this way, we will not get caught in the ego's trap of confusing form and content. He is, in the paradoxical term of the text, the "present memory" that links us back to the truth, and reminds us by its very presence that there is a love from which we never truly separated (T-28.I). When a loved one dies and the body is gone, for example, we are still linked by memories, thoughts, and symbols that remind us of the person. We thus remain connected and feel love or anger, depending on our state of forgiveness. It is as if the deceased were still here, because psychologically the person *is* here.

Thus the Holy Spirit—a memory or thought that symbolizes love— is the mediator that is described in "The Link to Truth" (T-25.I), the section from which I quoted earlier, mediating between the worlds of truth and illusion. He is spoken of as if He were a person, and we need to realize these are but symbols—helpful, but symbols nonetheless. As long as we see an image in our bathroom mirror every morning, and believe the image has a name—*our* name—and has a history—*our* history— we need a symbol to represent a non-ego presence in our minds. In *A Course in Miracles* this means Jesus or the Holy Spirit, Who remind us of God. We should certainly not stop asking for Their help, yet we need be aware that as we make our way on the journey home, we will increasingly recognize They are our Self, and we are Theirs. Yet, again, as long as we see ourselves as separate, we need a symbol of God that is also separate, which will lead us back to His unity.

He can do this because, while on the one hand He knows the truth, on the other He also recognizes our illusions, but without believing in them.

The Holy Spirit is the template of truth within our minds—a barometer if you will—to which we bring our experiences. It is that Thought that reminds us—by its very presence—that we are one. Whenever we are tempted to see others as different and separate from us, and feel justified in judging them for those differences, there is Someone within us to Whom we can bring those misperceptions. *A Course in Miracles* teaches us to bring illusions to the truth, separate interests to shared interests. The Holy Spirit is the great symbol of this truth, through Whom we learn to recognize our illusions. Thus whenever we experience another as different or separate, or a need that makes demands on others, we know we listen to the wrong teacher. Thus we can choose again and bring our ego's illusions to the Holy Spirit's truth.

It is the Holy Spirit's goal to help us escape from the dream world by teaching us how to reverse our thinking and unlearn our mistakes.

Remember, we are not speaking from the perspective of reality or knowledge. Within the dream, there is a process whereby we reverse our thinking and unlearn our mistakes. In the manual for teachers, Jesus talks about true learning in this world as unlearning (M-5.X.3:7). As we saw, the ego speaks first and is wrong. We need merely learn how wrong the ego has been, and how mistaken we have been in choosing it. Yet to unlearn what the ego has taught us, we first must learn *what* it has taught. That is why there is such a strong emphasis in the Course on understanding the ego's dynamics, especially the special relationship. How can we unlearn or choose against something when we do not know what we have learned or chosen? Our behavior is the effect of what we were taught, but we do not recognize that we taught ourselves, for the ego is nothing more than our self.

We can see, then, that the reason this is called *A Course in Miracles*, and comes in the curricular form of text, workbook, and manual for teachers is that we are in school. Moreover, the Course comes equipped with a specific curriculum—our special relationships—and provides a Teacher—the Holy Spirit or Jesus—Who helps in our study and practice. The Course, therefore, can be thought of as an educational system that teaches us about the ego thought system so that we can realize it is part of our mind. We learn it was not the world that taught separation to us, but the mind's decision to identify with the ego, a decision the mind then forgot and projected, so it now appeared as if the world—our parents, others, *A Course in Miracles*—were teaching us. However, there is no one out there to teach us! The world of separation is a world of illusion, and it is *we* teaching *us*; our insane self teaching itself an insane thought system that can now be corrected when this same self teaches us how. Our decision-making self does not teach what is positive, but rather undoes what is negative. When we unlearn the ego and it disappears, what remains is the memory of love, with which we now identify. This is the real world, at which point everything disappears.

The process, again, consists of unlearning our mistakes. This means we first have to realize we made them. Our parents, teachers, and religious and political leaders did not truly hurt us. We ourselves did that when we mistakenly chose the ego, and projected the mistake onto the world, which clearly may have abused and victimized us, not loved us as it should, was unkind, insensitive, and punitive. Yet the fact remains that we learned what we gave the world to teach us—not that others are not responsible for their egos, but these have nothing to do with our minds.

Returning to our earlier point, it is helpful to see how our lives fulfill the secret wish to keep our individual and special identities alive and well, and blame everyone else for them. No one or no thing made us neurotic, psychotic, or ill; our minds chose that, and then chose circumstances that would make it seem to everyone that our disturbance was justified: "Look what I grew up with! Look at the harsh hand fate dealt me!" It does not matter who or what did it, as long as it is someone or something other than ourselves. Thus we are not the dealer of the cards—we just sit at the table and they come. Yet they do not just "come"; we put them there, and deliberately forgot we did so. The Holy Spirit's role is therefore to be the Thought of sanity and truth, the perspective from which we look at our lives and realize that the secret of salvation is that we do this unto ourselves (T-27.VIII.10).

Forgiveness is the Holy Spirit's great learning aid in bringing this thought reversal about. However, the Course has its own definition

of what forgiveness really is just as it defines the world in its own way.

Forgiveness is the term that describes the thought reversal or un-learning of mistakes. It is not something we do, but *un*do; not we who forgive, but we who change our minds about what needs forgiveness—we forgive ourselves, not another. Jesus thus hints at how his course is unlike anything else, for it has its own definition of forgiveness. Similarly, the Course defines the world in its unique way, totally different from how the world sees itself. The universe of matter is literally a projection of the unreal thought of guilt, and because the world is seen differently, the process of its undoing must be different, too.

Projection Makes Perception

Paragraph 5

The world we see merely reflects our own internal frame of reference—the dominant ideas, wishes and emotions in our minds. "Projection makes perception" (T-21.in.1:1).

This is the first mention of *projection*. The phrase *the world you see* and its variants recur frequently in *A Course in Miracles,* and by it Jesus means literally the world *we* see, not just what the ego sees. He is not teaching that the world is real but the ego's interpretation is not—as some would like him to teach. Indeed, the Course says exactly the opposite: the world of perception and differentiation, beginnings and endings, is completely unreal. Since it is a place of change, it cannot be of God, Whose Heaven is unchanging—see, for example, "The Changeless Dwelling Place" (T-29.V) and "Changeless Reality" (T-30.VIII)—and what is not of God does not exist.

The "internal frame of reference" this world expresses is separation, and in fact the world of time and space is but the projection of the illusory thought of separation (space), and the equally illusory thought system of sin, guilt, and fear (linear time: past, present, and future). Despite the vastness of the cosmos, it remains an illusion that has never left its source in the mind. Thus the dominant wish the world reflects, as discussed above, is to make the separation a fact—to establish beyond question that our individual identity is real—and then avoid responsibility for it.

We look inside first, decide the kind of world we want to see and then project that world outside, making it the truth *as we see it*. We make it true by our interpretations of what it is we are seeing.

This is the process Jesus describes: We first look within and see sin, for which we avoid responsibility through projection—first onto God, and then the world. When we look with the ego—which is not really looking because we see what is *not* there—we see the sin of separation projected onto God, Who will destroy us. We thus protest it is not our fault: "We did not even eat a whole apple, only one measly bite, and God went ballistic. There was no choice but to hide in a world we had to make up." The inner world of separation—sin, guilt, and fear—projected out becomes the outer world, which we now regard as reality. A veil of forgetfulness then falls, separating the world from the mind's inner world, and we experience ourselves as bodies within the universe of materiality.

And so what our eyes show us is accepted as real, made true by our interpretation. We see a world that is hostile, cold, and threatening, and ourselves as weak, helpless, and vulnerable. As infants and children, that is certainly what we are, and as we grow, we become cruel and victimizing adults, an attitude justified on the basis of how cruel and victimizing adults treated us when we were young. We have therefore made a body that is weak, helpless, and vulnerable, alone in a hostile, threatening world with power to hurt us. All this seems real because we see it, and we see it because it fulfills our secret wish of being separate and not responsible. Finally, the veil drawn across our minds causes us to forget we made this up.

The motivation for such outward insanity is the ego's insane caution that if we look in the mind, we will be so overwhelmed by horror we would die. However, in truth, when we look within, we will merely double over in laughter because the ego is so preposterously silly. The thought we could destroy Heaven is as insane as an imperceptible ripple deciding it is the ocean, or a sunbeam asserting it is the sun (T.18.VIII.3:4). Looking at the mind with Jesus, we will see only this silliness. Therefore, because we do not want our separated selves to end, our egos decide not to look within, but without, believing that what we see is true.

We make it true by our interpretations of what it is we are seeing. If we are using perception to justify our own mistakes—our anger, our impulses to attack, our lack of love in whatever form it may take—we will see a world of evil, destruction, malice, envy and despair.

It is necessary to understand the distinction between seeing and perception. When Jesus says we "will see a world of evil, destruction, malice, envy and despair," he does not mean our physical eyes will *see* it, but that our mind will *think* it. This *is* a world of "evil, destruction, malice, envy and despair." Jesus makes very clear what this world is like, not to mention those who live in it. He says, for example, "frightened people can be vicious" (T-3.I.4:2), not that they are nice, sweet, or lovely. It is a fact within the perceptual world that people can be malicious and unkind, yet that does not make them evil or worthy of eternal damnation; nor does it exclude them from the Sonship. If that were so, we would be excluding everyone, for while most people may not act in cruel ways, everyone subscribes to cruel thoughts, because that was the nature of the original destructive thought of substituting ourselves for God. In this passage, therefore, Jesus speaks of what *we* make real—the power we give the ego over ourselves, others, and love.

The essential point is that there is a big difference between a perceptual fact—a fact within the dream—and our interpretation of that fact. In the manual for teachers, Jesus says,

> ...no one can be angry at a fact. It is always an interpretation that gives rise to negative emotions, regardless of their seeming justification by what *appears* as facts. Regardless, too, of the intensity of the anger that is aroused (M-17.4:1-3).

Thus we are angry at an interpretation of a fact, which may be that someone shot or raped me, or gave the order to drop a bomb on a million people. These are facts here, but they would not make me angry had I not first made a connection between what was done and me. The interpretation is that this person did this to me, or to someone or some group with whom I identify. The distinction is critical, and one that many students of *A Course in Miracles* miss, with unfortunate consequences. They will say, for example: "I do not want to watch a news program because I do not wish to see the terrible things that go on, which would contaminate my holy mind with evil." These students fail to see that they have already contaminated their minds, not because of

35

what goes on in the world, whether it is reported or not, but because they have made sin and evil real in themselves.

Absolutely nothing in *A Course in Miracles* is about the world, for it focuses exclusively on the mind and does not recognize the world's existence, as Jesus emphatically states: "There is no world! This is the central thought the course attempts to teach" (W-pI.132.6:2-3). Since the world is nothing but a shadowy projection of the mind's thought of separation and guilt, why would Jesus talk about a world that does not exist? He is not insane, and therefore he is concerned only with undoing the world of separation *in our minds*.

In this regard, the workbook says:

> The world was made as an attack on God.... [It] was meant to be a place where God could enter not ... (W-pII.3.2:1,4).

This is hardly a loving thought. Because we made the world to exclude God and His Love, we also made it to exclude everyone else, which means we feel guilty of the sin of excluding love by attacking it. Why, then, specify only certain forms of such attack? Yet that is what we do all the time. Recall the point about the early workbook lessons helping us see how much we exclude. Everyone is guilty of sin, otherwise no one would be here. The sinless do not flee Heaven and try to destroy it after leaving, but happily remain home with their Father.

Taking this as a given allows us to realize how we all walk the earth with the ego's cruel and wicked thought system in our minds. This realization makes the world quite boring, because everything is then seen as the same. The only mildly interesting things to notice are the ingenious ways in which we express that thought system, and the even more ingenious means we use to hide it. When the mind is healed and we are with Jesus in the holy instant, we see the same news programs, the same litany of atrocities that others see, but none of them disturbs the peace and love within.

Again, this has nothing to do with behavior. You may certainly act to stop the atrocities—you may run for public office, sign a petition or write a book, start a movement, or any number of things—but if you come from your right mind, there will be no anger or loss of peace. The minute, however, your peace is gone, so is sanity, which means whatever you believe, perceive, or say will be insane. This is why you should never listen to those who are angry or judgmental, for they no longer come from their right minds. It is not a sin to be angry, but it does distort your perception. The myth that angry people get things done has a certain amount of truth to it, just as the ego got things done at the beginning. Yet what they do is hardly loving. Is this what you really want?

What we do want to have done is what we *un*do, which occurs only with the miracle that is rooted in the Holy Spirit's Love. Perceiving an external problem with anger prevents the change of mind that is the miracle. External problems merely mirror the universal internal problem: when confronted with the choice between the ego and the Holy Spirit, we chose the ego. That alone is the problem, and its inevitable result is "a world of evil, destruction, malice, envy and despair." If we make such a world real by reacting to it, we aver that the mind's decision for the ego was correct. This means the Holy Spirit is an illusion, because it is always *one or the other*.

To state this one more time, we try to fulfill the ego's secret wish to keep its separate existence, but blame others—"using perception to justify our own mistakes." This harks back to the original mistake of choosing the ego instead of the Holy Spirit, from which comes "our anger, our impulses to attack, our lack of love." Projected guilt causes us to see evil, wickedness, and sin all around us. Yet this is what we want to see, so we can be justified in attacking and judging it. The way we know which teacher our minds have chosen is by paying attention to what we think and feel. Becoming either mildly annoyed or enraged —whether watching a news program, reading a newspaper, or in our daily interactions—witnesses to the choice for the ego. To accuse people of being malicious and evil, thereby giving them power over ourselves and others, is a red flag telling us we chose this for ourselves.

Our eyes will therefore see evil and cruelty, because this is the ego's world, but we need to learn not to give it power to take God's Love from us. Thus will our hearts open and embrace all people—victim and victimizer, oppressed and oppressor—because we realize there is no valid distinction among them. Either the totality of the Sonship is insane or sane; but it is *one or the other*, without gradation. Remember that the Preface began with this principle, and sanity and insanity have no in-between states. That is why the early lessons are so vital for the workbook's mind-training program: *Do not exclude.* We cannot include everyone on the level of form, but our minds can embrace the world without condemnation or judgment, if we so choose.

Forgiveness

All this we must learn to forgive...

Everything we see outside—the world of evil, destruction, malice, envy, and despair—we must learn to forgive. Jesus is not speaking of an abstract world, but the specific people we judge as evil, destructive, and malicious, whom we envy and despair over. And now we learn what it means to forgive:

...not because we are being "good" and "charitable," but because what we are seeing is not true.

Forgiving from our heart's goodness and charity is what Jesus describes in *The Song of Prayer* as *forgiveness-to-destroy* (S-2.I,II). Genuine forgiveness comes from recognizing that "what we are seeing is not true." Metaphysically speaking—Level One—what we see is not true because there is nothing here. However, this is not the level Jesus is addressing. He speaks to the selves who believe they exist as separated, autonomous beings. Here—Level Two—to say the evil "out there" has an effect on us is a lie, and this is where we move from the Course's metaphysics to its specific applications. It is a perceptual fact, once again, that people in the world can be cruel and deceptive, but our refrain should be: "What does that have to do with me?" Remember this earlier-quoted line:

> Let them be as hateful and as vicious as they may, they could have no effect on you unless you failed to recognize it is your dream (T-27.VIII.10:6).

The reason I am affected by what is happening is that I made it real. Yet the truth remains that nothing has the power to take away my peace. *Nothing.* On a practical level, we need to watch how we give that power to everyone and everything. We can give it to a little ant that upsets us, or to a head of state who wages war on another country, thereby sending us into fits of rage or terror. It can be something that seems gargantuan in its scope, or minor and trivial. If it upsets our peace—if we see ourselves separated from that ant or head of state, or a family member or colleague—it is because we first decided to separate from the Love of God, and then projected our "sin," blaming someone else. Perception is the outward picture of an inner wish

(T-24.VII.8:8-10), which we have kept secret. It has remained in the mind, but we do not know it is there because we wanted to hide it.

We have distorted the world by our twisted defenses, and are therefore seeing what is not there.

I accuse myself of separating from the Love of God, label my act sinful, and experience the guilt that demands punishment. Projecting the guilt, I see a world poised to attack, betray, and abandon me. Once I have accorded reality to this perception, I put on the face of innocence—because of what is done to me, I have to defend myself (T-31.V.2-3). I ultimately need a defense because I believe I will be destroyed by Heaven. Thus a twisted defense develops to protect a twisted sense of self—"the home of evil, darkness and sin" (W-pI.93.1:1). Yet that is not my true Self, for I am the home of light, peace, and joy (W-pI.93), albeit covered by the ego's self-concept. Seeking to preserve this self, I project it onto others and blame them for my pain. A veil falls, as discussed above, and I forget *I* did this. I do not see evil, darkness and sin in a decision *I* made, but see it rather in you and the world around me. Seeing no connection between what I perceive outside and what I made real inside, I justify my attacking it. Jesus tells us the unforgiving thought "protects projection" (W-pII.1.2:3), and as long as I hold an unforgiving thought against you, justifying it by getting dozens, thousands, or millions to agree with me that you are the evildoer, I do not remember I projected it—the unforgiving thought is thus protected by seeing it in someone else.

Although Jesus tells us we are "seeing what is not there," he is not asking us to deny what our body sees or feels, or what other bodies feel; nor is he implying that we should not respond to our bodily needs. But he is asking us to deny the connection we made between what another is doing—however cruel that may be—and our peace of mind. This is an inherent aspect of the principle *projection makes perception*. Jesus teaches us not to give what another person does the power to take away our peace and love, which embrace all people as the same. This is what it means to practice the Course, whether we do it in the context of the workbook for one year, or for a lifetime.

Whenever we do not feel peaceful and at one with the Sonship—not in a quasi-mystical state, but recognizing our collective misery—we know we have chosen the ego. Learning this is why we are asked to pay attention to our world, and is the meaning of the Holy Spirit's third lesson—to be vigilant only for God and His Kingdom (T-6.V-C)—which emphasizes the need to be vigilant for the ego so we may remember God's Kingdom. We therefore watch ourselves as we do something trivial, drive on the freeway, or make life-changing decisions; observe our reactions at work, with our families, or in relation to a current event. We do not judge or evaluate these reactions, but merely watch. The chances are that nine hundred ninety-nine times out of a thousand we will give something external the power to disrupt our peace: something will "make us" anxious, angry, depressed, fearful, happy, ecstatic, feel pleasure or pain. Again, it is essential that we not judge ourselves for this—we are here solely to learn from a new teacher a different way of perceiving these experiences.

The essence of *A Course in Miracles*, therefore, is that we learn to shift our focus from the world, where we placed it—our own and others' bodies—to the mind. At first this is difficult because we are not even aware we have a mind. That is why we need a teacher and a course that continually repeats the same message. This helps us understand that we can look differently at the relationships and situations we are in, seeing them as projections of the mind's decision.

As we learn to recognize our perceptual errors, we also learn to look past them or "forgive."

"Forgive" is in quotes because Jesus is defining *forgiveness* as looking past perceptual errors. In many places in the Course, he uses the word *beyond*, wherein we see beyond or overlook the ego. This does not mean, however, that we do not see the ego. We do see the error, not realizing at first what it is, which leads us to respond with specialness. Eventually recognizing the mistake, we go within, asking Jesus' help to look at the situation differently. This shifts the focus from what is outside to the decision-making mind. We come to understand that the perceptual error is not what the eyes see or ears hear, but that we have given power to our sensory organs to take away our peace: I was so happy five minutes ago and then you entered the room, telephoned me, I read your letter, or I turned on the news—I was fine, but all of a sudden, through no fault of my own, I am hurt, plunged into despair or on the verge of committing homicide. Yet all these reactions come from a connection that does not exist, for how can what is not here truly affect us? Nothing can affect us here because nothing can touch our minds. Needless to say, this takes much training and practice, dedication and vigilance, because we made the world and body to do exactly the opposite: to keep us mindless and blame other bodies for our pain.

A recurring phrase in the *I Ching*—a profound compendium of Chinese wisdom—is "no blame." Everything here, however, *is* blame. Our birth is blame, as is a crying infant, expressing the mind's secret wish to be adversely affected by the world so we can blame the external. Thus we are justified in erecting defenses to protect ourselves against external threat. Perception deceives, however, because it was made to bring us information of unfair treatment. In "The Attraction of Guilt," Jesus describes how the ego trains "hungry dogs of fear" and sends them to pounce on any trace of guilt or sin, bringing to their master what they find (T-19.IV-A.12-15). We are all these ravenous dogs, poised to pounce on others, either to cannibalize because we think we love them, or murder because we think we hate them. We need to accept that there is something in us sending out these vicious messengers, kept starving for guilt so they will be motivated to find the sin in another that ensures the ego's salvation.

Returning to the idea that forgiveness looks beyond the ego, we need to be clear about Jesus' intention. He does not want us to bypass the ego in ourselves or others, but truly to look at it, which we do until we can smile from within. This smile gently corrects our having taken the ego seriously, when we believed not only that it was real, but that it had real effects on us or others. The smile says our mistake was silly, and this is the meaning of looking with Jesus. He always "smiles"— the gentle laughter he describes in this wonderful passage:

> In gentle laughter does the Holy Spirit perceive the cause, and looks not to effects. How else could He correct your error, who have overlooked the cause entirely? He bids you bring each terrible effect to Him that you may look together on its foolish cause and laugh with Him a while. *You* judge effects, but *He* has judged their cause. And by His judgment are effects removed. Perhaps you come in tears. But hear Him say, "My brother, holy Son of God, behold your idle dream, in which this could occur." And you will leave the holy instant with your laughter and your brother's joined with His (T-27.VIII.9).

This is clearly not a derisive laughter that makes fun of others, but a gentle smile that in effect says the situation is not serious. Within the dream it well might be, but outside it—in the healed mind—the world has no power. And so we look with Jesus as the ego's granite wall of sin dissolves, with nothing remaining but a flimsy veil with no power to keep away the light (e.g., T-18.IX.5; T-22.III.3-5). Thus we look "beyond" by looking at the ego. In fact, the miracle is defined as looking at the ego's devastation:

> It merely looks on devastation, and reminds the mind that what it sees is false (W-pII.13.1:3).

Needless to say, we cannot see the ego's falsity until we look at it. Note that Jesus does not say look on beauty and love, but rather devastation, that we may learn that what we see is false, as the healing thought of Atonement smiles gently at our illusions.

At the same time we are forgiving ourselves...

This is a key theme in the Course. As I forgive you I forgive myself, because God's Son is one. What I forgive in you is a projection of what is unforgiven in me; what I secretly hold against you I secretly hold against myself. And so I can never have a judgmental thought about you without first having projected my own guilt. By looking past your guilt—which means seeing it and then asking for another way to look at it—I do the same for myself, for it is the same guilt. We need not be at home with the Course's metaphysics that says there is literally no one out there—such awareness comes only at the journey's end—for all we need know now is that our accusations of another reflect our accusations of ourselves. By thus excluding another from the Sonship—accomplished by anger and judgment—we exclude ourselves, because God's Son is one.

Remember that the Course's definition of *Heaven* is "an awareness of perfect Oneness" (T-18.VI.1:5-6). Truth in the world's dream *reflects* that Oneness, which means that God's Son is not only one in spirit as Christ, but also as a split mind: we share the same insanity of believing we would be better off leaving Heaven and inhabiting the "rotting prison" of a body (T-26.I.8:3). This is madness, and all who think they are bodies—saints *and* sinners—are equally mad, thinking the body is real, and what they do with another body will make them feel better, or make the world a better place. Yet how could we make the world or body a better place? We left the better place! Instead, we need to return home and not try to improve the illusion, which but reinforces the ego's strategy of making it real.

At the same time we are forgiving ourselves, looking past our distorted self-concepts to the Self that God created in us and as us.

That Self is one. If we seek to exclude one person—forget about millions—whose abuse of us or others we will never forgive, and we carry that around like an albatross, as in Coleridge's "The Rime of the Ancient Mariner," that is sufficient to sustain the spot of guilt that says the separation is reality. Thus Jesus says in his glorious final vision:

> …and not one spot of darkness still remains to hide the face of Christ from anyone (T-31.VIII.12:5).

If one person is kept apart from the Sonship, all have been, including ourselves and Jesus. As yet, we do not know we have done this to ourselves, and so we begin by paying attention to our special relationships. When we let these grievances go, realizing no one can make us happy or unhappy, we become more peaceful and thus can accept the truth of forgiveness Jesus teaches in his course.

Special Relationships

What follows is a two-paragraph statement of special relationships, the heart of the ego thought system. To recap our journey so far, we began in Heaven's perfect Oneness, continued through the separation and the world of perception that opposes knowledge, and arrived in the dream. We also discussed how perception arose from the projection of the mind's thought system of separation, and are now ready to explore this thought system in more depth, and its manifestations in our special relationships.

Paragraph 6

Sin is defined as "lack of love" (T-1.IV.3:1). Since love is all there is, sin in the sight of the Holy Spirit is a mistake to be corrected, rather than an evil to be punished.

I have likened this Preface to a musical prelude that introduces many of the themes that will follow. A prominent theme in *A Course in Miracles* (see, for example, "Sin Versus Error" and "The Unreality of Sin" [T-19.II,III]) is that errors or mistakes are corrected, while sins are punished. When I accuse someone of doing something reprehensible or unkind, I am hardly smiling; yet my ego is because the sinner has been identified. I therefore need to ask for help to smile and not take the form of attack seriously. I thus learn from my new teacher that viciousness comes from a thought system of guilt and fear, which is also my thought system and everyone else's. With this insight, all I wish is to embrace the fear and touch its pain with the gentle hand of forgiveness—the shift from perceiving a sin to be punished, to a mistake to be corrected. This cannot happen as long as I harbor sin within myself.

We need to keep in mind that the way we perceive the world is the result of how we perceive ourselves. Consequently, if we do not change our self-perceptions, we cannot change our perceptions of the world. That is why it is important to look at the world and our reactions to it, bringing those reactions to Jesus and understanding his words that the world is "the outside picture of an inward condition" (T-21.in.1:5). He later says that perception is "the outward picture of a wish; an image that you wanted to be true" (T-24.VII.8:10). We thus begin to understand that the world exists for the right-minded purpose of being the mirror of what we have projected from ourselves, providing the means of returning to it. Once that is accomplished, we look back on the world and see it as does the Holy Spirit: containing expressions of love or calls for it. As we discussed before, it makes no difference which we see, because either way our response is loving, having nothing to do with the decisions or behaviors of another. The burden for our well-being is thus shifted from external circumstances to the mind—the process of forgiveness that removes the burden of guilt we placed onto ourselves and others.

Our sense of inadequacy, weakness and incompletion comes from the strong investment in the "scarcity principle" that governs the whole world of illusions.

As I mentioned in the Introduction, this is the only place in the material where the term *scarcity principle* appears, although the concept is present throughout. This principle says that I separated from God, and because I banished love and my real Self, there is a gaping hole within me that I can never fill. The best I can do is steal from the outside to fill what is lacking. Since love is what is missing, I steal it, learning at an early age how to manipulate, seduce, and control so that people will love me: be attracted to me and pay attention to my needs; be faithful, kind, and sensitive; and be there on demand. It goes without saying that I do not truly care about them, but only that my suffering be alleviated.

The pain of our lack is so excruciating that all we can ever think of is filling it, but to no avail, for this is the black hole of guilt in which love disappears and is never heard from again. It is no accident, therefore, that astronomers are fascinated by their recent discovery of black holes, which reflect the ego's black hole we keep filling, though it is never enough. We continually indulge ourselves with one special relationship after another in a process that is unending, just as our need for food, drink, and oxygen can never be satiated. No one avoids this here, because it is the world's nature never to satisfy. Our bodies reflect this lack, for they always fight physical and psychological emptiness. Continually in need of filling itself, the body is one colossal black hole— a gaping mouth that seeks only to cannibalize, even as it causes the external to vanish. And because the fill is transitory, we forever struggle with feelings of inadequacy, powerlessness, and incompletion, driving us to put more and more into our bodies. Incidentally, this is the ultimate source of addictions, regardless of their form. The ego naturally loves all this, because our obsession with filling the emptiness camouflages the *whole* that is really in us. When we identify with that whole—the wholeness of Christ—we see no one here as different or separate from us; in form, yes, but in content we are the same—part of Christ, and part of the separated Son of God.

Finally, notice Jesus' words: "the strong investment in the scarcity principle." We all are invested in maintaining the scarcity that governs the world, and everything here represents an attempt to fill what is missing. This, then, answers the question of why we choose to be unhappy and in pain: it is *we* who suffer. This *we* is our investment—we may be miserable, but we exist, and are perversely willing to pay the price of pain and suffering as proof of this existence. The crumb the ego offers for our pain is that at least we will be off the hook. The world is demonstrably terrible, but our suffering shows it is not our fault. This is the picture of crucifixion we offer to another: "Look what you did. You crucified, humiliated, and betrayed me." People indeed behave horrendously, yet on an unconscious level we relish every agonizing minute because our pain sees to it that another will pay the cost of our life. And so Jesus tells us we would not even find death too great a price to pay, if it allows us to say: "Behold me, brother, at your hand I die" (T-27.I.4:6).

From that point of view, we seek in others what we feel is wanting in ourselves. We "love" another in order to get something ourselves.

The love that I feel is absent in me is in you, and it comes in many forms—romantic, sexual, filial, friendship, admiration, etc. The form makes no difference, as long as I get the attention my ego craves. I love you because of what I get from you, which leads to the special relationship bargain: Since I must pay for what I get, I must figure out what it will cost me. When people meet for the first time, they size each other up, whether consciously or not. How do I get this person to like me, give me a job, grade me highly on my paper, or marry me? We determine what others need, and then supply it; all the while they do the same with us. The special relationship bargain is ugly, deceptive, and painful, but it works. Yet its real success lies in keeping love away, because love is not based on need but abundance. This love naturally extends and embraces everyone, taking whatever form is appropriate and helpful. Many forms of love exist in our world, but only their content of all-inclusiveness is important.

That, in fact, is what passes for love in the dream world. There can be no greater mistake than that, for love is incapable of asking for anything.

This implies the concept of need, which governs all existence. Our ultimate need is to protect our individual selves by blaming others, the basis for the special love bargain. It is not really that I bargain with you to get what I want. In truth, I am setting you up so you will *not* give me what I want, for then I entrap you in my ego's lair. I hang your sins high so everyone, including God, will see. Thus do people fail us, which proves beyond a shadow of a doubt that we are the innocent ones. Following the principle of *one or the other*, they become the guilty sinners. In fact, the more crushed and devastated we are, the better our chances of winning the ego's Oscar. We excel as actors and actresses, and nowhere do we shine more brilliantly than when we suffer. Victimization is not a pretty picture, but it gets us what we want: to keep our separate and special identities, but with someone else paying the price of sin. It is a masterful strategy, and the world of bodies is its insane fulfillment.

The ego tells us at the beginning that separation—our separate selves—is equated with sin. It then reveals its plan to save us: "All you need do," it says, "is worship at my altar and pledge allegiance to me." It seeks to have us keep the separation we stole and get rid of the sin. Thus we make a world of multiplicity in which there are a quasi-infinite number of objects onto which we can project our sin, enabling us to keep our separate selves, but be sinless—sin-less, because someone else now has it. This is the essence of the malicious special relationship —the ego's maladaptive way of joining with others—only hinted at here. We think we are being loving, but in reality we but steal and cannibalize, as we believe we once did to God. This discussion leads us to the next paragraph, which teaches that is not bodies that join. As the text states: "Minds are joined; bodies are not" (T-18.VI.3:1).

Paragraph 7

Only minds can really join, and whom God has joined no man can put asunder (T-17.III.7:3).

This quote from the text comes from the well-known line in Mathew's gospel (19:6), which the Catholic Church used to declare divorce a sin. In *A Course in Miracles*, this has a totally different meaning, having nothing to do with form—the Church's emphasis— but with content. God has joined us as one Son, united with Him, and the ego cannot separate what is His Will. In its delusional system the ego thinks it can, but not in reality.

It is, however, only at the level of Christ Mind that true union is possible, and has, in fact, never been lost.

True oneness exists only in Heaven, on the level of spirit—the Christ Mind. What is possible here, once again, is to reflect that oneness by recognizing we are joined in sharing a common interest and need. As already discussed, this should not be taken to mean that we deny our bodies, existing only as one glorious mass of protoplasmic love. It is much more helpful to learn that we simply share the same thought systems of hate and forgiveness.

The "little I" seeks to enhance itself by external approval, external possessions and external "love."

This, incidentally, is the only place in *A Course in Miracles* where the term "little I" is used for the ego.

We know the word *external* is key here for it is stated three times. It refers to the body and the perception of someone out there—our special partners in love and hate. As part of the scarcity principle, we have already judged ourselves to be nothing. We then attempt to enlarge this puny and inadequate self by getting approval and love from others, and acquiring bigger and better things—all because we feel so empty inside. There is nothing wrong with having possessions, but when we have a *need* for them, and feel elated when we get them or disappointed when we do not, that is the clue this is the ego's doing. We somehow think we will feel different when we get that bigger and better job, car, house, or family. *Bigger and better* is the name of the ego's game, and it does not matter what it is. When we feel good because we have acquired something external, it is but the ego's ploy to compensate for the "little I" that feels puny, weak, and insignificant. We magically hope that by attaching to something outside us, we will become a larger "I," without having to change ourselves. Growing through relationships with others is how we learn—think of children, for example—but when there is no growth but only stealing, we have fallen into the ego's snares of specialness. Inevitably, we end up devastated because the guilt over our sin has been reinforced.

The Self that God created needs nothing. It is forever complete, safe, loved and loving. It seeks to share rather than to get; to extend rather than project. It has no needs and wants to join with others out of their mutual awareness of abundance.

The essential point, again, is *needs*. When we are as God created us, we have no needs. Yet here, everyone is needy; that is why we came. If we do not feel guilty because we breathe and eat, we should not feel guilty because we want to steal from another. There is no difference. This is certainly not to suggest that we feel guilty when we breathe; but if we do not, we should also not feel guilty because we cannibalized someone else to satisfy our need for specialness. The ego, after all, cannot help its cannibalism; it is a huge, gaping mouth. We need only be aware of it, without trying to spiritualize, justify, or deny it. We look at the ego with Jesus beside us and see the insanity that is its source. Above all, we realize the ego's thought system does not work, for this will eventually enable us to let it go. The hole of scarcity is never filled, as we have seen, for only the Love of God will satisfy us.

Paragraph 8

The special relationships of the world are destructive, selfish and childishly egocentric.

This covers almost everyone: "destructive, selfish and childishly egocentric." We care only about ourselves and the satisfaction of our needs, and are nice as long as others meet them. When they cease to do so, however, we cast them aside without a second thought— "another can be found" (W-pI.170.8:7) as we embark "on an endless, unrewarding chain of special relationships." (T-15.VII.4:6). Yet although these relationships are hateful, we are not asked to change them or let them go, but only to look without judgment, as the next passages will tell us.

The Holy Relationship

Jesus now eases the pain of special relationships by speaking of their counterpart, the holy relationship. Keep in mind that just as the special relationship is only with the ego thought system, the holy relationship has nothing to do with another person, but with the Holy Spirit. My attempts to cannibalize you are simply the projections into form of what my mind has done with the ego, as my forgiveness reflects the decision for the Holy Spirit, Whose principle of shared interests symbolizes God's Oneness. If this is misunderstood, we will inevitably be stuck in a morass of the specialness of form, and think it is wonderful and holy.

Yet, if given to the Holy Spirit, these relationships can become the holiest things on earth—the miracles that point the way to the return to Heaven.

A beautiful line in "For They Have Come" says: "The holiest of all the spots on earth is where an ancient hatred has become a present love" (T-26.IX.6:1). This holy spot is not external, but is in the mind that has chosen to return home, where the ego's ancient hatred becomes the Holy Spirit's present love. This love expresses itself in forms—relationships with people—but these are illusory, being extensions of love rather than the love itself. The miracle—its first mention in the Preface—is the Course's name for this correction.

What changes, therefore, is not the relationship between two bodies, but the relationship the mind has with its teacher, translated into the purpose given to our relationships. Beforehand, the special relationship had as its purpose the bringing of bodies awash with the blood of murder to the ego's altar—using others as scapegoats so we would end up innocent and they guilty. When we realize this does not work, the purpose can shift, so that relationships no longer serve as battlegrounds on which we defeat others by having them defeat us, but as classrooms in which we follow a different Teacher. Thus we perceive in our special relationships the projections of our special relationship with the ego, allowing us to shift the purpose from its guilt to the Holy Spirit's forgiveness.

The world uses its special relationships as a final weapon of exclusion and a demonstration of separateness.

We could add to that, "and a demonstration of my innocence." I exclude you because you are evil, and my hurt demonstrates we are separate. However, it is your fault because I was so kind, loving, and sweet, one with you until you attacked me. It does not matter whether it is something silly like not taking out the garbage, or a serious offense like declaring war or abusing a child.

The Holy Spirit transforms them into perfect lessons in forgiveness and in awakening from the dream.

Recall that in the text Jesus explains how the Holy Spirit does not take away our special relationships, but transforms them, shifting their purpose (T-15.V.5; T-17.IV.2:3; T-18.II.6-7). This really means He does nothing, for *we* are the ones who shift the purpose. *A Course in Miracles*, again, is written on the dualistic level we can accept and understand, and so the language describes the Holy Spirit as active, but in reality He just *is*, as God *is*. His Love, like a lighthouse, shines out, and we bring to it the darkness of our illusions. The excruciating pain of our guilt motivates us finally to cry out "there must be another way!"—and then everything changes.

Each one [special relationship] **is an opportunity to let perceptions be healed and errors corrected. Each one is another chance to forgive oneself by forgiving the other. And each one becomes still another invitation to the Holy Spirit and to the remembrance of God.**

When we turn to Jesus, he helps us look at our special relationships differently. While each had been a source of tremendous pain, we now see it as a projection, an outward picture of an inward state—the secret wish to be separate and blame someone else for it. And now we can say and mean that we no longer want this. The relationship becomes holy because its purpose is not to root us and others still further in the dream, but to help us awaken from it. The ego's dream is one of separation, guilt, and blame, but having accepted the dream's new purpose, we realize others have not done anything to take away our peace. Their behavior might have been unconscionably wicked and cruel, but that had no real effect on us. Not one note in our song of love was missed (T-26.V.5:4) because of what others said or did. Their seeming sin had no effect, and thus I forgive myself for having believed it did. Therefore, it is not really the special ones I forgive, but myself.

The invitation to the Holy Spirit comes when I recognize, as did Helen and Bill, that "there must be another way." The pain of my special relationships is intolerable, which means my decision for the ego is too painful. I thus appeal to my decision maker when I say: "Please choose again." The other choice is for the Holy Spirit, the remembrance of Who I truly am. As God's Son I am whole, and in that wholeness all are healed because we are one—if my mind is healed, all minds are healed (W-pI.137). Others may choose not to accept the healing, but in my mind the Atonement is complete. There is no one left to forgive or heal, for to recognize all are one means there is no separation, which is how I remember I never left God.

This principle of the healing of one mind being the healing of all minds is why we say that *A Course in Miracles* is meant only for one person—*you*. Whoever the *you* is who studies and applies the Course is its audience. When your mind is healed, you know—not only intellectually—that God has only one Son. That makes no sense on this side of the veil, but in the right mind, where the separation is healed, you understand there is but one student and one Teacher. There is no one to convince, convert, or preach to. This, again, does not mean the body does nothing. It simply means you know that what motivates your body—behavior, thoughts, and words—is love.

To return to our earlier point, the focus of *A Course in Miracles* is not to make the world a better place, for how can we make an illusion better? Even more to the point, why would we want to? Other spiritualities may have this as a goal, but the Course's unequivocal emphasis is on having the *mind's* world become a happier place. As our minds become forgiven of their guilt and judgments, the ego loses its power and dissolves, leaving in its stead the memory of God's Love—the Holy Spirit. At this point, anything the body says or does reflects His Love and principle of shared interests. The form may not seem like that, but love's content is unchanging. The real world—the goal of forgiveness—is not Heaven on earth, but the state of mind where there is no ego. Thus we realize there is no world to save because the mind of God's Son has been healed—the separation has been undone. Now with Jesus outside the dream, we know we are not here, even though our bodies appear to be. Therefore, nothing is to be done, for we have no investment in the body's activity—ours or another's. Jesus' love alone is our focus.

We can also see here what amounts to a formula in *A Course in Miracles*: You see the face of Christ in your brother, and remember God. The face of Christ—not talked about here—is a symbol of innocence. It is of course not a face, for it is not something your eyes see; it but expresses the vision we shall talk about presently. To see the face of Christ is to withdraw the projections of sin you put onto another, bringing them back to yourself. This means the person is sinless. The process begins with your belief another was sinless and you sinful. Projecting this belief gave rise to the magical belief you were without sin, now found in the other. When you withdraw the sin from the projected image, you allow that person's innocence to shine forth. Once the darkness of sin is brought to the light within, you recognize you are innocent, too.

Forgiveness, therefore, originates in the pain we feel from still one more special relationship. However, this time we blow the whistle on the ego and say we have had enough—since specialness does not work, we no longer wish to tolerate its pain. Help comes through shifting our perception and purpose for the relationship. These shifts are what the Course refers to as *happy dreams*, a term not used in the Preface. These have nothing to do with anything external, but reflect the mind's right-minded state when we have undone the seeds of unhappiness: sin, guilt, and attack—the ego's nightmares of separation.

Mind and Body

As I mentioned at the beginning, this part of the discussion can be likened to a musical intermezzo or interlude. It speaks of the relationship between body and mind, connecting to the previous discussion of perception before its segue into vision. The relationship between mind and body is central to an understanding of *A Course in Miracles*. In one sense, this theme is the Course's central focus, because it helps us move from our experience as bodies to the mind, where both problem and answer are found.

Paragraph 9

Perception is a function of the body, and therefore represents a limit on awareness.

Perception involves an elaborate sensory apparatus. Organs sensitive to external stimuli bring back sensory data to the brain, which then interprets them. It is a drastic limit on awareness, because the body is itself a limit, as the text states: "the body *is* a limit on love" (T-18.VIII.1:2). If love is all there is and we are limiting it—really, burying it—how can we possibly be aware of anything? In the ego's arrogance, we think we are very aware; yet what we are truly seeing is nothing. We think it is something, and then invent theories and explanations to make sense of the data our deceiving sensory organs bring back to us. Many passages throughout the Course's three books speak of this perceptual deception.* In some of them Jesus pokes gentle fun, saying we see with eyes that do not see, hear with ears that do not hear, and think with brains that do not think.

Jesus thus means his words literally. As we read them, we feel we understand and even accept them, but then go about our daily business still believing we are thinking, seeing, and hearing. Again, the information we perceive is drastically limited—and even that is an overstatement. Yet in our madness we think it reports reality. As Jesus

---

* See, for example, T-28.V.4; T-28.VI.1-2; W-pI.92.1-3; M-8.3-4.

says to us in the text, we ask the one thing in the world that does not know—the ego and body—to tell us what reality is (T-20.III.7). We then come up with theories—from physics, chemistry, astronomy, biology, psychology, sociology, economics, theology, and philosophy—that strive to make sense of the data our sensory organs brought to us. Yet these "perceptual facts" are all made up, which is exactly the ego's goal.

Perception sees through the body's eyes and hears through the body's ears. It evokes the limited responses which the body makes. The body appears to be largely self-motivated and independent, yet it actually responds only to the intentions of the mind.

When the body responds to the mind's intentions, there are but two possibilities: the ego, whose intention is to perpetuate separation and project the blame for it; or the Holy Spirit, Whose intention is to awaken us from the separation and blame no one for it. Yet the body was made to be self-motivated, for it seems to carry within itself its own motivation, having genes that either determine or predispose our body and emotions to be a certain way. In fact, everything physical and emotional is explained through the body, which thus belies the mind's primacy.

If the mind wants to use it [the body] for attack in any form, it becomes prey to sickness, age and decay.

In other words, we become sick, grow old, deteriorate, and ultimately die, because that is the mind's wish. The body, therefore, does not dictate its own conditions, and there are no *natural* physical or developmental laws. Our minds make these laws, for it is our dream, and we follow them as if they were independent of us. This is the meaning of: "The body appears to be largely self-motivated and independent." Yet in truth the body is not independent of our decision. After making the laws, the mind sets them into motion and then causes us to forget itself. And so the laws appear to have lives of their own, as, for example, with the laws of genetics. Again, the problem is not a specific law, but the mind that set it into motion. However, at any moment we can choose again.

As an illustration, let us say I put my car in neutral, take my foot off the brake and hands off the wheel as it rolls down a hill toward an embankment. What accounts for the inevitable catastrophe is my setting the car in motion and removing my foot and hands from the brake and wheel. Unimpeded, the car does what any machine would do under those circumstances. Without interference or resistance, it rolls until it meets its tragic end, while I sit claiming I cannot stop the car. However, I do have a foot and hands that are sitting idly by, allowing the crash to occur. That is our situation. Our minds set the ego in motion, make the world and body that hurtle toward destruction, while Jesus calmly says to us: "Put your foot on the brake and hands on the wheel. You have a mind that can stop all this." Yet we play dumb and say: "What foot? What brake? What mind?"

This, then, is the message of *A Course in Miracles*: reminding us we have within us the means to stop our "engines of destruction" (T-20.VIII.4:8). Jesus has given us his course to describe how and why the cars of our bodies were made, how we sit helplessly by, complaining of our cruel fate. We gather momentum as we speed downhill toward the cliff of death, and yet stubbornly maintain we can do nothing about it. However, Jesus keeps telling us that we can do something. We have feet and hands that can stop the car, if only our minds would give the order. There is no reason, he would tell us, that we have to re-enact the movie *Groundhog Day*, wherein we keep repeating the same day over and over and over again. We insist we cannot stop the cycle, yet Jesus thinks otherwise (T-23.I.2:7), asking us to turn to him for help so the pain and destruction can be averted. Yet we choose not to listen, for we want the car to fall off the precipice so we can maintain the tragedy is not our fault: someone put us in the car, pushed it, and set the precipice in front of us.

Still speaking of the body, Jesus continues:

If the mind accepts the Holy Spirit's purpose for it [the body] instead, it becomes a useful way of communicating with others, invulnerable as long as it is needed, and to be gently laid by when its use is over.

Note that Jesus is not talking about living forever in the body. He teaches that death is a decision, as is sickness, being born, feeling good, growing old—indeed all physical life. The body responds only to the mind's intentions, and since we do not know what or where the mind is, it is difficult to comprehend Jesus' teaching. Thus he shows us the mind's effects—indirect teaching is necessary because direct truth is still too threatening (T-14.I.2,5).

To say this is a course in miracles is saying this is a course in re-training perception, for the miracle is a perceptual shift. Rather than seeing outward, we take what our eyes have seen and bring it to the mind, so we may learn, as we have seen, that the world is "the outside picture of an inward condition" (T-21.in.1:5). Yet we exclaim: "What inward condition?" Since all we know is the outer world of bodies and know nothing of a mind, we cannot really understand Jesus' words. Moreover, we do not want to. He thus needs to motivate us, as must all teachers; otherwise students will not learn. By Jesus showing us the pain of our lives—misery, frustration, and despair—we are motivated finally to seek change. Fear, however, keeps us denying the simple truth of our situation, and so we assert how wonderful everything is—especially since we found this wonderful course, for which we say: "Thank you, Jesus, but please do not make us understand what you teach."

Because we all want some form of magic, we must understand that nothing here works, and so we cannot in all honesty blame the world, the body, or others. We need to realize that we are sitting in the car, fully capable of stopping it from racing over the precipice. Yet the ego has us see the body as vulnerable, doomed to a life of suffering that culminates in death, yet all the while we hold everyone and everything else responsible. The Holy Spirit, however, perceives the body as a communication device through which He teaches us about the mind. In other words, He sees the world and body as classrooms, but it remains our choice what they will teach us, as we now read:

Of itself it [the body] is neutral, as is everything in the world of perception. Whether it is used for the goals of the ego or the Holy Spirit depends entirely on what the mind wants.

A lesson in the workbook is entitled "My body is a wholly neutral thing" (W-pII.294). Once the body was made for a non-neutral purpose —to limit love and attack God—it can serve either as a prison from which there is no escape, or a classroom that helps set us free. The choice is ours. When Jesus says *mind*, therefore, he refers to the decision maker. Indeed, this is all he ever speaks of, because there is nothing else in the dream. Recall that the decision-making mind chooses between two thoughts—the ego's separation, guilt, and hate; or the Holy Spirit's Atonement, forgiveness, and love—both of which do nothing. The decision maker does the work of changing; the two thoughts remain what they are. The mind's choice is thus predicated on the purpose we want: to sleep or to awaken. Our desire determines our teacher, which in turn determines how we perceive the world.

This leads us to the final part of the Preface, which focuses on the vision of forgiveness.

True Vision

Paragraph 10

The opposite of seeing through the body's eyes is the vision of Christ, which reflects strength rather than weakness, unity rather than separation, and love rather than fear.

The ego wants us to see separate bodies, which is why our senses were made. I said before that separation, differences, judgment, and attack are really one and the same: We see *separate* bodies, and *judge* the *differences* for purposes of *attack*. Thus, some bodies are nice, others are not; some are holy; others are not. We attack by dividing people into special love and special hate categories. The body's eyes see only this because that is what the ego sent them to see—the "hungry dogs of fear" that perceive separation and then attack the differences that judgment feeds on. When such perceptions become too painful, we cry out: "Stop! There must be another way, another teacher, another way of looking." This is the shift from the ego's judgmental seeing to Christ's forgiving vision.

With vision, the body's eyes see as they always have, for nothing changes on the external level. The change occurs with the mind's interpretation. Thus our eyes continue to see separation and differences, physical symptoms and attack, but we no longer judge them, realizing that the differences we see are superficial. They mean nothing because everyone's mind is the same: the ego's thought system of 100 percent guilt, hate, suffering, and death; the Holy Spirit's thought system of 100 percent forgiveness, healing, peace, and love; and the decision maker that chooses between them. The thought systems never change, only the decision maker. Some choose to spend more time in one part of the mind than the other, but we all share the same mind. This is the meaning of the New Year's prayer in the text, "Make this year different by making it all the same" (T-15.XI.10:11), which reflects Christ's vision that expresses His strength, Heaven's unity, and God's Love. Vision is not oneness or love, but since it does not perceive judgment —the interpretation of physical differences that makes them real—the inherent sameness it does perceive reflects Heaven's unity. With sin, guilt, and fear gone, only the memory of God's Love remains in our healed minds.

It is helpful to read passages like these and watch our response. There is a part of each of us that would say: "I do not want to let these grievances go. I do not want to let go of being right, even if it means sacrificing my happiness." This honest appraisal of where we are means we would not attempt to defend against these feelings. This opens the mind's closed door, and allows us to look within with Jesus and ultimately choose his loving strength.

The opposite of hearing through the body's ears is communication through the Voice for God, the Holy Spirit, which abides in each of us.

Not only do sin, guilt, and fear abide in each of us, but so does the Holy Spirit. What the body hears is thus transformed to "hearing" through the right mind.

His Voice seems distant and difficult to hear because the ego, which speaks for the little, separated self, seems to be much louder.

This theme of the ego's raucous shrieking drowning out the still, small voice of the Holy Spirit recurs in the Course itself. One of the more striking passages from the text asks how we could possibly hear the Holy Spirit's Voice when all we listen to is the voice of specialness —separation, differences, judgment, and attack:

> What answer that the Holy Spirit gives can reach you, when it is your specialness to which you listen, and which asks and answers? Its tiny answer, soundless in the melody that pours from God to you eternally in loving praise of what you are, is all you listen to. And that vast song of honor and of love for what you are seems silent and unheard before its "mightiness." You strain your ears to hear its soundless voice, and yet the Call of God Himself is soundless to you (T-24.II.4:3-6).

How could it be the Holy Spirit speaking when you judge others? It is indeed the voice of the holy spirit you hear, but it is the ego's spirit of holy judgment to which you listen. God's Holy Spirit never judges, and if you accentuate differences instead of the inherent sameness of God's Son, it is not Heaven's Voice you pay attention to, no matter how profound the experience might seem. The ego is quite subtle, and can sound very much like the Holy Spirit. Yet anything that puts a barrier between you and even one person is not the voice of love, which never excludes. Thus the Voice for God seems distant only because you prefer the song of specialness in its place.

Returning to our image of the car hurtling to its demise, Jesus sits beside us, encouraging us to awaken from the dream. He is "still, and quietly does nothing.... [He] merely looks, and waits, and judges not" (W-pII.1.4:1,3). He speaks words of comfort and wisdom, even as we choose not to hear. Needless to say at this point, this is metaphorical, for Jesus does not truly speak. His non-specific love does not use words—there are none in the real world—but our minds and brains shape it into a form we can accept and understand: shared instead of separate interests.

This is actually reversed. The Holy Spirit speaks with unmistakable clarity and overwhelming appeal. No one who does not choose to identify with the body could possibly be deaf to His messages of release and hope, nor could he fail to accept joyously the vision of Christ in glad exchange for his miserable picture of himself.

The problem is our identification with the body. If we do not identify with this ego prison, we cannot but hear the Holy Spirit's Voice, for It is ever present in our minds. However, if we continue to choose the voice that speaks to the body, we will never hear the Holy Spirit. Again, His Voice does not truly speak, for He knows not of bodies, which do not exist. Thus He knows the difference between appearance and reality, dreams and truth. The Holy Spirit is unmistakably clear and has tremendous appeal because His is the Call for Love, referred to in the text as "The Attraction of Love for Love" (T-12.VIII). It is love for itself, because love is one; we just think it is two. It is very important to understand that Heaven's Voice "speaks" to us constantly (W-pI.49), but we actively choose not to hear It. As one Son, we made a deliberate choice at the beginning to turn from the Holy Spirit's Atonement that said the separation never happened. If we never separated from God, *we* never happened. We thus listened instead to the ego's voice, which said: "A wonderful thing has occurred—*you*. The separation is real, and so are you."

In that ontological instant we were confronted with a choice, and as one Son we chose. It was a no-brainer. We chose the ego because we liked being separated, differentiated, independent, and special, and so we chose not to hear the Holy Spirit. From that point on His Voice was buried in our minds, covered by the ego's thought system of guilt, which in turn was covered by the world of guilt—a double shield of oblivion (W-pI.136.5:2): the shield of the world shrouding the guilt in darkness; the shield of guilt shrouding the love in darkness. Love is not truly in darkness, however; it is merely veiled, and at any given moment we can lift the veil. Yet we refuse, because the ego's voice warns we will disappear into the Heart of God, which means annihilation and oblivion. We thus choose not to listen, and the core of Jesus' course is that if we choose *against* the Holy Spirit, we can just as easily choose *for* Him. The choice is ours, but we need learn we have a mind that can exercise this power.

As we ride in the ego's car, racing headlong to our death, we are taught we can do something about it. Yet we resist the truth, because part of us wants to be right—to die and blame others. We all are born into this suicidal car called the body, and know at some point it will fall over the precipice. This perversely insane thought system to which we cling is fine with us, because it will not be our fault. However, all the time, again, Jesus is there, gently reminding us that we can stop this madness whenever we choose. Yet we have turned the ego's radio up so loud we do not hear, for we would much rather listen to the ego's raucous shrieks of dissonance so that we become upset and angry. Anything but listen to the still, small Voice, gently saying: "My brother, choose again." We flee from this as from the plague, and continue to pursue the ego's futile cycle of specialness—life, pain, death; life, pain, death.

Though we drive different model cars, a common end is inevitable for us all—the body dies, and we accusingly take as many with us as we can. But Jesus waits, and because he is not in time, his patience is infinite (T-5.VI.11:6). Only when the pain becomes unbearable do we ask for help, and he explains that all we need do is put our foot on the brake and the ego will stop. Our suffering, therefore, is important, for it supplies the needed impetus to change and alleviate the mind's pain. That is why the text states that the Holy Spirit wants us to be aware of our misery, because He cannot teach without that awareness (T-14.II.1). He contrasts the misery of pain with joy, because we have them backwards—what the ego thinks of as joy is really pain. Jesus therefore asks us to see the distinction between the ego's insanity and his sanity, so we can make a meaningful choice.

Paragraph 11

Christ's vision is the Holy Spirit's gift, God's alternative to the illusion of separation and to the belief in the reality of sin, guilt and death.

Once we choose the ego and forget we did so, there is seemingly no available alternative for we muted the Holy Spirit's Voice. It is not truly gone, but has become inaccessible as long as we maintain the decision to keep our separate self and make others responsible for it. In exchange for Christ, we have chosen a self that is the home of sin, guilt, and fear, the parody and travesty of the glorious Self God created one with Him (T-24.VII.1:11; 10:9). This grotesque ego self masquerades as a body, its home of certain death. We need to see this was our choice, and one we still make. We see here, incidentally, the power of *A Course in Miracles* as our pathway home, for at the same time Jesus speaks on a high spiritual level, he also clarifies how we are to live his teachings in our everyday lives.

It is the one correction for all errors of perception; the reconciliation of the seeming opposites on which this world is based.

We must humbly accept that we are wrong about everything we see, because our perception reflects separation, differences, judgment, and attack. There is in truth only one error—separation—and only one solution—the miracle. The error manifests here as separate interests, and the solution as shared interests.

A key word here is *seeming*. There are no true opposites, for there is nothing here to oppose. This is an alternative to Jung's theory that is predicated on the notion that reconciling opposites is the foundation of individuation: we are made whole by reconciling the opposites within—good and evil. Yet this rests on the belief that good *and* evil are real, and must be accepted as such in ourselves. There is certainly a therapeutic value in this process, for denial of self—wrong or right mind—merely reinforces the ego's illusion. However, this "reconciliation" will not awaken us from the dream of duality. Opposites are but appearances, and the way good and evil are truly reconciled is through realizing they are both illusory, brought about by perceiving people as not opposite or different, but the same in interest and goal. What alone is opposite are the thought systems of the ego and Holy Spirit, and when you bring the ego's darkness of guilt to the Holy Spirit's light of love, the ego disappears. Moreover, we have seen that as the ego disappears, so does the Holy Spirit because He is the correction and the answer. Once the problem has been corrected and the question answered, the need for the Holy Spirit is gone.

Along with the "opposites" of good and evil, there are God and the ego, spirit and flesh. Remember, however, that *A Course in Miracles* is not dualistic. That is why these are referred to as *seeming* opposites. There is no point in reconciling what does not exist, but we need to look at both polarities and move beyond them to Christ's unifying vision, for judgment and true perception are the only meaningful opposites within a world of illusion. Once again, when we bring the darkness to the light, both dissolve into the blazing truth on the mind's decision-making altar—guilt, forgiveness, and the altar disappear, leaving only Heaven's knowledge as the reality beyond the ego's world of opposites:

> And now God's *knowledge*, changeless, certain, pure and wholly understandable, enters its kingdom. Gone is perception, false and true alike. Gone is forgiveness, for its task is done. And gone are bodies in the blazing light upon the altar to the Son of God. God knows it is His Own, as it is his. And here They join, for here the face of Christ has shone away time's final instant, and now is the last perception of the world without a purpose and without a cause. For where God's memory has come at last there is no journey, no belief in sin, no walls, no bodies, and the grim appeal of guilt and death is there snuffed out forever (C-4.7).

Its [vision's] kindly light shows all things from another point of view, reflecting the thought system that arises from knowledge and making return to God not only possible but inevitable.

Remember, Christ's vision is an illusion, for it only symbolizes Heaven's Oneness. Still, it is the final illusion, undoing all others and reflecting the unified thought system that arises from knowledge—the unchanging, eternal Self. From another point of view, therefore, vision illuminates the perceptual world of separation, but representing shared interests, not selfish, independent, or divided ones. Thus Jesus asks us in the workbook, and throughout the Course, to practice his teachings quite specifically. It is helpful to observe how rarely we come from the perception that sees everyone as the same—not the *form,* for example spending equal time with everyone, or loving all in the same way; but the *content* that does not exclude nor judge against those whom we are not with. In this way, vision's kindly light "shows all things from another point of view."

When Helen and Bill joined together in a holy instant, setting aside their separate interests—Bill saying there must be another way, and Helen agreeing with him—they shared one purpose. This made *A Course in Miracles* possible, the answer they asked for. They fought about everything except the Course, for they were able to set their egos aside and share the purpose of bringing it into the world. This is the other point of view to which Jesus refers. It reflects the oneness that arises from knowledge, which we could not choose if its memory were not already within our split minds. That is why return to God is not only possible but inevitable. Yet we need to remember that to make this happen, we must be aware of how much we do not want to make this happen, for such awareness ensures that we will ultimately accept the means of its accomplishment.

"Returning to God" means awakening from the dream, and the miracle of forgiveness is the means: seeing shared instead of separate interests. It cannot be said often enough how essential it is that we be aware of our judgments. Instead of hearing people's calls for help and their pain, we choose to judge, attack, and find fault, clogging our ears so that we will not hear the cries of anguish. When we do allow ourselves to hear, we recognize that pain is in everyone—good and bad, victims and victimizers. This is what Christ's vision shows us and the Holy Spirit's Voice tells us. Thus we "see" and "hear" people's calls for help, and our hearts go out to them all.

A Course in Miracles leads us to this experience, so each day is shaped by Christ's vision. And so we do not empathize with the perceived agony of others, but touch their true pain with the gentle hands of forgiveness. Pain's source is the awareness—albeit unconscious— that we are in a world in which we know we do not belong, yet not knowing our true home. We know nothing but the body's rotting prison, symbolized by the car that heads full-speed for the precipice, still fearful of the voice that explains how to prevent the inevitable. Specifically, Jesus teaches that the vehicle of death is stopped by seeing everyone in the car with us, and he pleads with us to overcome our resistance to his vision of all people calling out for the love they do not believe they deserve.

What was regarded as injustice done to one by someone else now becomes a call for help and for union. Sin, sickness and attack are seen as misperceptions calling for remedy through gentleness and love.

Nothing changes but the interpretation of our sensory data. Despite the distortions of our sensory apparatus, we look through Christ's vision and exclude no one from our forgiveness. Perceiving injustice in ourselves or others tells us we have listened to the wrong voice, for the Holy Spirit teaches us to see in sickness and attack only calls for help and union, expressing the pain that cries out: "Please help. I know how to escape pain only through attack, yet that yields only more pain. Please show me another way." We could be that helping person if we choose to, but we will not hear the cry of pain as long as we embrace our own so we can blame someone else.

For sure, our very existence depends on pain, which is why we cling to it with a tenacity that is almost boundless. Since bodies were made to feel pain to distract from the mind's pain of guilt, Jesus emphasizes throughout the Course that bodies do not suffer. They feel nothing, like the lifeless pieces of wood we call puppets. The mind gives the body a message that says: "Feel pain so you can say: 'Behold me, brother, at your hand I die.'" Thus we are instructed to suffer pain, an easy price to pay as long as God will punish another for our sin. Read, for example, these searing words from near the end of the text:

> If you can be hurt by anything, you see a picture of your secret wishes. Nothing more than this. And in your suffering of any kind you see your own concealed desire to kill (T-31.V.15:8-10).

We want God to destroy our brothers as punishment for their sins, and our wounds are proof they did this to us. We gladly suffer now so redemption will be ours later when they are dispatched to hell. Because it is *one or the other*, when God takes them He will spare us. We then get as many people as possible to witness to God on our behalf so

He will feel for our abuse, humiliation, and betrayal. Perceptions of injustice, fortified by our suffering, thus become a primary defense in the ego's arsenal against our choosing to return home.

Defenses are laid down because where there is no attack there is no need for them.

Recall our earlier discussion that defenses are present because we believe we have to defend the little self we think we are. We feel vulnerable to attack because this self came into existence by attack, and we must defend it from itself. Since all we know is attack, which began our troubles, our most meaningful defense is attack. This is the foolproof nature of the ego system, for within itself there is no way out of these quasi-endless cycles of hate: I get rid of my painful guilt by attack, which makes me even guiltier, and so I attack again; furthermore, I inevitably feel I will be attacked in return, requiring defense, and so the guilt-attack cycle leads to the attack-defense cycle—when I attack you, I believe you will attack me back; whether you do so or not is irrelevant, I believe you will. And so guilt leads to attack, which leads to defense, which constitutes attack and more guilt. We keep recycling this insane and vicious thought system until the pain becomes so unbearable that we cry out for help.

This help comes through our realizing what is truly happening, and deciding we no longer want it. But first we must feel the pain of having identified with the ego, for otherwise we will not let it go. As a subtle form of resistance, we try to strike a bargain with Jesus, trying to minimize the pain yet retaining the ego's thought system of separation. This will not work. Only experiencing the discomfort of our judgments —having to prove others wrong so we can be right—will open us to the other way of looking. Jesus thus helps us see that attack is not salvation; being right does not make us happy; pushing people into the mud of guilt merely pushes us into the same mud; and cannibalizing and manipulating others so they will give us what we want does not bring us joy. There may be a momentary sense of exultation and triumph because we have won—again!—but this is met by almost instantaneous guilt that demands we replay the specialness game. Recognizing the futility of pursuing special relationships is all the motivation we need to choose against them.

Our brothers' needs become our own, because they are taking the journey with us as we go to God.

This line provides a wonderful summary of our daily practice of forgiveness. Our brothers cannot go without us, and we cannot go without them. In other words, our needs are the same: theirs are ours; ours are theirs. It is the same need because we come from the same thought. We are but seeming fragments of a seamless whole—an insane whole to be sure, but seamless for we remain one within the illusion of fragmentation. What gets us back on the right journey with the right teacher is understanding we are our sameness—the good and bad thieves; the sheep and the goats; those who understand *A Course in Miracles* and those who do not. Everyone travels the same journey in content. However, we need to see how much we do not want certain people on the journey; not only that we do not want to have dinner with them, but we do not want them to return home with us. However, Jesus helps us understand that if they do not return, neither do we. It is thus in our best interests to take everyone with us because everyone *is* with us; indeed, everyone *is* us. If we deny this fact and seek to justify our denial by rationalizing attack and injustice, we will lose our way and pain is unavoidable.

Jesus tells us in the text:

> You have no idea of the tremendous release and deep peace that comes from meeting yourself and your brothers totally without judgment (T-3.VI.3:1).

It is equally true that we have no idea of the pain that comes from holding on to judgment. That is why peace feels so wonderful: the pain has stopped. We must realize, as the text says, that we walk home "together, or not at all" (T-19.IV-D.12:8). "Together" is not just ourselves and our brother—the object of our special love or special hate—but anyone we seek to exclude at any time.

Without us they [our brothers] would lose their way. Without them we could never find our own.

It is those we most want to exclude who are our saviors, because we have projected our "secret sins and hidden hates" (T-31.VIII.9:2) onto them. We placed in those we hate the guilt we had buried in the mind's vault, and therefore they offer us the opportunity of seeing what we kept hidden from the light. All we need do is be aware of how much we do not want to let our projections go. We need do nothing else—not heal ourselves, attempt to be holy, or envision making the journey with all our brothers. Rather, we need to see ourselves *not* wanting to make such a journey, because the truth is we are already on the journey with them. Our focus, therefore, need be on removing the interference to that awareness, and so we should visualize how much we do not want people to come with us, and then be able to forgive ourselves. Jesus' role is to help us not attack our decision to reject him as our teacher, and our not wanting him to invite everyone with us as we go. If we could forgive these judgments, our hardness of heart would disappear and we would know that all truly walk with us—we happily did not have to bring our brothers; we merely opened our eyes so we could see them. Thus are they helped to see, too.

Paragraph 12

Forgiveness is unknown in Heaven, where the need for it would be inconceivable.

This is another major tenet of the Course's teachings. We read in the workbook, for example:

> God does not forgive because He has never condemned (W-pI. 46.1:1).

Forgiveness is the correction for our having chosen the ego, wherein we forgive the illusions of separation, which do not exist in Heaven.

However, in this world, forgiveness is a necessary correction for all the mistakes that we have made.

Our mistakes are one mistake—the thought we are better off on our own, killing to meet our selfish needs: the principle of *one or the other*. Forgiveness helps us realize this is the premise of everyone's life, and it does not make us feel good or bring us happiness. How could it? Life on a battleground is not happy, safe, restful, or peaceful, for one must always be vigilant for the enemy. Yet it is *our* battleground, *our* dream, *our* enemy, born of *our* sin. However, since it is our own, we can change it—the message forgiveness would have us learn.

To offer forgiveness is the only way for us to have it, for it reflects the law of Heaven that giving and receiving are the same.

Giving and receiving are the same because I give only to myself and receive only for myself (W-pI.126). If I give you sin, I reinforce it in me because it is my sin I give you, having first made it real in my mind. However, if I extend forgiveness, it is because I perceive no sin in me and therefore perceive none in you. Remember, *projection makes perception*. If, however, I "forgive" your sin and still retain my belief in it, I have forgiven nothing; i.e., *forgiveness-to-destroy*. Forgiveness is true only when it embraces all, without exception. If anyone is excluded—including ourselves—it cannot be forgiveness because it does not correct the ego's thought of separation.

Heaven is the natural state of all the Sons of God as He created them. Such is their reality forever. It has not changed because it has been forgotten.

This expresses the Atonement principle, even though the word itself does not appear. Heaven has not been affected because we forgot about it, nor has the oneness of the Sonship changed; moreover, we still walk home together even though our eyes are closed. Thus, when Jesus says that "Heaven is the natural state of all the Sons of God," he refers to our oneness—there are no Sons of God, only God's *one* Son. The illusion of many remains because our world is one of multiplicity. Yet the illusion gently disappears into the one as we practice with each seemingly separate person, realizing our interests are not separate but the same.

Chapter 3

THE JOURNEY'S END: THE FORGIVEN WORLD

Paragraph 13

The final paragraph is a lovely conclusion to the Preface. It brings together everything we have discussed, culminating with the forgiven world, the title of a beautiful section in the text (T-17.II). The forgiven or real world is attained when the ego has been totally undone and we have accepted the Atonement for ourselves. We are led there by realizing we walk with everyone, the only true fact within the dream. Choosing to accept the Atonement was the mind's only real choice, and having made it, we enter into the forgiven world, resting but an instant at Heaven's gate while the dreams of guilt, forgiveness, and the journey itself disappear, leaving only the Love we never left. Here, now, is the closing paragraph, which ends the Preface as it ends our preparatory journey for *A Course in Miracles*:

Forgiveness is the means by which we will remember. Through forgiveness the thinking of the world is reversed. The forgiven world becomes the gate of Heaven, because by its mercy we can at last forgive ourselves. Holding no one prisoner to guilt, we become free. Acknowledging Christ in all our brothers, we recognize His Presence in ourselves. Forgetting all our misperceptions, and with nothing from the past to hold us back, we can remember God. Beyond this, learning cannot go. When we are ready, God Himself will take the final step in our return to Him.

APPENDIX

HOW IT CAME

A Course in Miracles began with the sudden decision of two people to join in a common goal. Their names were Helen Schucman and William Thetford, Professors of Medical Psychology at Columbia University's College of Physicians and Surgeons in New York City. They were anything but spiritual. Their relationship with each other was difficult and often strained, and they were concerned with personal and professional acceptance and status. In general, they had considerable investment in the values of the world. Their lives were hardly in accord with anything that the Course advocates. Helen, the one who received the material, describes herself:

> Psychologist, educator, conservative in theory and atheistic in belief, I was working in a prestigious and highly academic setting. And then something happened that triggered a chain of events I could never have predicted. The head of my department unexpectedly announced that he was tired of the angry and aggressive feelings our attitudes reflected, and concluded that, "there must be another way." As if on cue, I agreed to help him find it. Apparently this Course is the other way.

Although their intention was serious, they had great difficulty in starting out on their joint venture. But they had given the Holy Spirit the "little willingness" that, as the Course itself was to emphasize again and again, is sufficient to enable Him to use any situation for His purposes and provide it with His power.

To continue Helen's first-person account:

> Three startling months preceded the actual writing, during which time Bill suggested that I write down the highly symbolic dreams and descriptions of the strange images that were coming to me. Although I had grown more accustomed to the unexpected by that time, I was still very surprised when I wrote, "This is a course in miracles." That was my introduction to the Voice. It made no sound, but seemed to be giving me a kind of rapid, inner dictation which I took down in a shorthand notebook. The writing was never automatic. It could be interrupted at any time and later picked up again. It made me very uncomfortable, but it never seriously occurred to me to stop. It seemed to be a special assignment I had somehow, somewhere agreed to complete. It represented a truly collaborative venture between Bill and myself, and much of its significance, I am

sure, lies in that. I would take down what the Voice "said" and read it to him the next day, and he typed it from my dictation. I expect he had his special assignment, too. Without his encouragement and support I would never have been able to fulfill mine. The whole process took about seven years. The text came first, then the workbook for students, and finally the manual for teachers. Only a few minor changes have been made. Chapter titles and subheadings have been inserted in the text, and some of the more personal references that occurred at the beginning have been omitted. Otherwise the material is substantially unchanged.

The names of the collaborators in the recording of the Course do not appear on the cover because the Course can and should stand on its own. It is not intended to become the basis for another cult. Its only purpose is to provide a way in which some people will be able to find their own Internal Teacher.

WHAT IT IS

As its title implies, the Course is arranged throughout as a teaching device. It consists of three books: a 669-page text, a 488-page workbook for students, and a 92-page manual for teachers. The order in which students choose to use the books, and the ways in which they study them, depend on their particular needs and preferences.

The curriculum the Course proposes is carefully conceived and is explained, step by step, at both the theoretical and practical levels. It emphasizes application rather than theory, and experience rather than theology. It specifically states that "a universal theology is impossible, but a universal experience is not only possible but necessary" (manual, p. 77). Although Christian in statement, the Course deals with universal spiritual themes. It emphasizes that it is but one version of the universal curriculum. There are many others, this one differing from them only in form. They all lead to God in the end.

The text is largely theoretical, and sets forth the concepts on which the Course's thought system is based. Its ideas contain the foundation for the workbook's lessons. Without the practical application the workbook provides, the text would remain largely a series of abstractions which would hardly suffice to bring about the thought reversal at which the Course aims.

74

The workbook includes 365 lessons, one for each day of the year. It is not necessary, however, to do the lessons at that tempo, and one might want to remain with a particularly appealing lesson for more than one day. The instructions urge only that not more than one lesson a day should be attempted. The practical nature of the workbook is underscored by the introduction to its lessons, which emphasizes experience through application rather than a prior commitment to a spiritual goal:

> Some of the ideas the workbook presents you will find hard to believe, and others may seem to be quite startling. This does not matter. You are merely asked to apply the ideas as you are directed to do. You are not asked to judge them at all. You are asked only to use them. It is their use that will give them meaning to you, and will show you that they are true.
>
> Remember only this; you need not believe the ideas, you need not accept them, and you need not even welcome them. Some of them you may actively resist. None of this will matter, or decrease their efficacy. But do not allow yourself to make exceptions in applying the ideas the workbook contains, and whatever your reactions to the ideas may be, use them. Nothing more than that is required (workbook, p. 2).

Finally, the manual for teachers, which is written in question and answer form, provides answers to some of the more likely questions a student might ask. It also includes a clarification of a number of the terms the Course uses, explaining them within the theoretical framework of the text.

The Course makes no claim to finality, nor are the workbook lessons intended to bring the student's learning to completion. At the end, the reader is left in the hands of his or her own Internal Teacher, Who will direct all subsequent learning as He sees fit. While the Course is comprehensive in scope, truth cannot be limited to any finite form, as is clearly recognized in the statement at the end of the workbook:

> This Course is a beginning, not an end...No more specific lessons are assigned, for there is no more need of them. Henceforth, hear but the Voice for God...He will direct your efforts, telling you exactly what to do, how to direct your mind, and when to come to Him in silence, asking for His sure direction and His certain Word (workbook, p. 487).

INDEX OF REFERENCES TO *A COURSE IN MIRACLES*

text

Foundation for A COURSE IN MIRACLES®

Kenneth Wapnick received his Ph.D. in Clinical Psychology in 1968 from Adelphi University. He was a close friend and associate of Helen Schucman and William Thetford, the two people whose joining together was the immediate stimulus for the scribing of A COURSE IN MIRACLES. Kenneth has been involved with A COURSE IN MIRACLES since 1973, writing, teaching, and integrating its principles with his practice of psychotherapy. He is on the Executive Board of the Foundation for Inner Peace, publishers of A COURSE IN MIRACLES.

In 1983, with his wife Gloria, he began the Foundation for A COURSE IN MIRACLES, and in 1984 this evolved into a Teaching and Healing Center in Crompond, New York, which was quickly outgrown. In 1988 they opened the Academy and Retreat Center in upstate New York. In 1995 they began the Institute for Teaching Inner Peace through A COURSE IN MIRACLES, an educational corporation chartered by the New York State Board of Regents. In 2001 the Foundation moved to Temecula, California, and shifted its emphasis to electronic teaching. The Foundation publishes a quarterly newsletter, "The Lighthouse," which is available free of charge. The following is Kenneth's and Gloria's vision of the Foundation.

In our early years of studying *A Course in Miracles,* as well as teaching and applying its principles in our respective professions of psychotherapy, and teaching and school administration, it seemed evident that this was not the simplest of thought systems to understand. This was so not only in the intellectual grasp of its teachings, but perhaps more importantly in the application of these teachings to our personal lives. Thus, it appeared to us from the beginning that the Course lent itself to teaching, parallel to the ongoing teachings of the Holy Spirit in the daily opportunities within our relationships, which are discussed in the early pages of the manual for teachers.

One day several years ago while Helen Schucman and I (Kenneth) were discussing these ideas, she shared a vision that she had had of a teaching center as a white temple with a gold cross atop it. Although it was clear that this image was symbolic, we understood it to be representative of what the teaching center was to be: a place where the person of Jesus and his message in *A Course in Miracles* would be manifest. We have sometimes seen an image of a lighthouse shining its light into the sea, calling to it those passers-by who sought it. For us, this light is the Course's teaching of forgiveness, which we would hope to share with those who are drawn to the Foundation's form of teaching and its vision of *A Course in Miracles*.

This vision entails the belief that Jesus gave the Course at this particular time in this particular form for several reasons. These include:

1) the necessity of healing the mind of its belief that attack is salvation; this is accomplished through forgiveness, the undoing of our belief in the reality of separation and guilt.

2) emphasizing the importance of Jesus and/or the Holy Spirit as our loving and gentle Teacher, and developing a personal relationship with this Teacher.

3) correcting the errors of Christianity, particularly where it has emphasized suffering, sacrifice, separation, and sacrament as being inherent in God's plan for salvation.

Our thinking has always been inspired by Plato (and his mentor Socrates), both the man and his teachings. Plato's Academy was a place where serious and thoughtful people came to study his philosophy in an atmosphere conducive to their learning, and then returned to their professions to implement what they were taught by the great philosopher. Thus, by integrating abstract philosophical ideals with experience, Plato's school seemed to be the perfect model for the teaching center that we directed for so many years.

We therefore see the Foundation's principal purpose as being to help students of *A Course in Miracles* deepen their understanding of its thought system, conceptually and experientially, so that they may be more effective instruments of Jesus' teaching in their own lives. Since teaching forgiveness without experiencing it is empty, one of the Foundation's specific goals is to help facilitate the process whereby people may be better able to know that their own sins are forgiven and that they are truly loved by God. Thus is the Holy Spirit able to extend His Love through them to others.

Responding in part to the "electronic revolution," we have taken the Foundation's next step in our move to Temecula, California. With this move to a non-residential setting we are shifting our focus, though not exclusively, from totally live presentations to electronic and digital forms of teaching in order to maximize the benefits of the burgeoning field of electronic media communication. This will allow us to increase our teaching outreach, the *content* of which will remain the same, allowing its *form* to adapt to the 21st century.

Related Material on
A Course in Miracles

By Kenneth Wapnick, Ph.D.

Books

(For a complete list and full descriptions of our books and audio and video publications, please see our Web site at www.facim.org, or call or write for our free catalog.)

Christian Psychology in *A Course in Miracles*. Second edition, enlarged.
ISBN 0-933291-14-0 • #B-1 • Paperback • 90 pages $5
Audio version of the second edition of the book, read by Kenneth Wapnick • #T2 $10

Translation available in Spanish.

A Talk Given on *A Course in Miracles*: An Introduction. Seventh edition.
ISBN 0-933291-16-7 • #B-3 • Paperback • 131 pages $6

Translations available in Spanish, Portuguese, German, Dutch, French, Danish, Italian, Slovene, and Afrikaans.

Glossary-Index for *A Course in Miracles*. Fifth edition, revised and enlarged.
ISBN 0-933291-03-5 • #B-4 • Paperback • 349 pages $10

Translations available in Spanish and German.

Forgiveness and Jesus: The Meeting Place of *A Course in Miracles* and Christianity. Sixth edition.
ISBN 0-933291-13-2 • #B-5 • Paperback • 399 pages $16

Translations available in Spanish and German.

The Fifty Miracle Principles of *A Course in Miracles*. Fifth edition.
ISBN 0-933291-15-9 • #B-6 • Paperback • 107 pages $8

Translations available in Spanish and German.

Awaken from the Dream. Second edition. Gloria and Kenneth Wapnick.
ISBN 0-933291-04-3 • #B-7 • Paperback • 132 pages $10

Translations available in German and Spanish.

The Obstacles to Peace.
ISBN 0-933291-05-1 • #B-8 • Paperback • 295 pages $12

Love Does Not Condemn: The World, the Flesh, and the Devil According to Platonism, Christianity, Gnosticism, and *A Course in Miracles*.
ISBN 0-933291-07-8 • #B-9 • Hardcover • 614 pages $25

A Vast Illusion: Time According to *A Course in Miracles*. Second edition.
ISBN 0-933291-09-4 • #B-10 • Paperback • 345 pages $12

    Translation available in German.

Absence from Felicity: The Story of Helen Schucman and Her Scribing of *A Course in Miracles*. Second edition.
ISBN 0-933291-08-6 • #B-11 • Paperback • 498 pages $17

    Translation available in German.

Overeating: A Dialogue. An Application of the Principles of *A Course in Miracles*. Second edition.
ISBN 0-933291-11-6 • #B-12 • Paperback • 70 pages $5

A Course in Miracles and Christianity: A Dialogue. Kenneth Wapnick and W. Norris Clarke, S.J.
ISBN 0-933291-18-3 • #B-13 • Paperback • 110 pages $7

    Translations available in Spanish and German.

The Most Commonly Asked Questions About *A Course in Miracles*. Gloria and Kenneth Wapnick.
ISBN 0-933291-21-3 • #B-14 • Paperback • 144 pages $8

    Translations available in Spanish, German, and Dutch.

The Message of *A Course in Miracles*. Volume One: *All Are Called*. Volume Two: *Few Choose to Listen*.
Two Volumes: 619 pages
ISBN 0-933291-25-6 • #B-15 • Paperback $22 (set)

    Translations available in Spanish and German.

The Journey Home: "The Obstacles to Peace" in *A Course in Miracles*.
ISBN 0-933291-24-8 • #B-16 • Paperback • 510 pages $16.95

Ending Our Resistance to Love: The Practice of *A Course in Miracles*.
ISBN 1-59142-132-2 • #B-17 • Paperback • 94 pages $5.00

Life, Death, and Love: Shakespeare's Great Tragedies and *A Course in Miracles*. Four-volume set based on *King Lear, Hamlet, Macbeth,* and *Othello*.
Four Volumes: 383 pages
ISBN 1-59142-142-X • #B-18 • Paperback $25 (set)

The Healing Power of Kindness—Volume One: Releasing Judgment.
ISBN 1-59142-147-0 • #B19 • Paperback • 109 pages $6.00

The Healing Power of Kindness—Volume Two: Forgiving Our Limitations.
ISBN 1-59142-155-1 • #B20 • Paperback • 118 pages $6.00

Form versus Content: Sex and Money.
ISBN 1-59142-194-2 • #B21 • Paperback • 116 pages $7.00

Journey through the Workbook of *A Course in Miracles*. Commentary on the 365 lessons.
Eight Volumes: 1,158 pages
ISBN 1-59142-206-X • #B-23 • Paperback $60 (set)

Ordering Information

For orders *in the continental U.S. only,* please add $6.00 for the first item, and $1.00 for each additional item, for shipping and handling. The shipping charge for *Journey through the Workbook of A COURSE IN MIRACLES* is $10.00; add $1.00 for each additional item.

For orders to *all other countries* (SURFACE MAIL), and to *Alaska, Hawaii,* and *Puerto Rico* (FIRST CLASS MAIL), please add $6.00 for the first item and $2.00 for each additional item. The shipping charge for *Journey through the Workbook of A COURSE IN MIRACLES* is $10.00; add $2.00 for each additional item.

California State residents please add local sales tax.

VISA, MasterCard, Discover, American Express accepted.

Order from:

Foundation for A COURSE IN MIRACLES
Dept. B
41397 Buecking Drive
Temecula, CA 92590
(951) 296-6261 • FAX (951) 296-5455
Visit our Web site at *www.facim.org*

* * * * *

To order additional copies of this book, send a check or money order (in US funds only) for $7.00 plus shipping to the above address; please see shipping charges above.

A Course in Miracles and other scribed material
may be ordered from:

Foundation for Inner Peace
P.O. Box 598
Mill Valley, CA 94942
(415) 388-2060

A Course in Miracles, Second Edition, Complete:
Hardcover - 6" x 9": $35
Softcover - 6" x 9": $30
Paperback - 5" x 8": $20

Psychotherapy: Purpose, Process and Practice: $6

The Song of Prayer: Prayer, Forgiveness, Healing: $6

The Gifts of God: $21

Concordance of *A Course in Miracles*: $49.95

Foundation for A Course in Miracles®
Dept. B
41397 Buecking Drive
Temecula, CA 92590

☐ I am interested in receiving a newsletter

☐ I am interested in receiving a catalog of publications

☐ I am interested in receiving a schedule of workshops and classes

☐ Place me on your mailing list to receive your catalog and quarterly newsletter

PLEASE PRINT NEATLY

Name _____

Address _____

City, State, Zip _____